CW00349123

A TIME TO SERVE

CARMEL FENNESSY

A Time to Serve

Loitering with Intent

ST PAULS

Cover illustration by: Michelle – a prisoner.

ST PAULS Publishing
187 Battersea Bridge Road, London SW11 3AS, UK
www.stpauls.ie

Copyright © Carmel Fennessy 2002

ISBN 085439 631 4

Set by TuKan DTP, Fareham, UK
Printed by CPI Bath

ST PAULS is an activity of the priests and brothers
of the Society of St Paul who proclaim the Gospel
through the media of social communication

To my niece and godchild, Jill

The names used are not necessarily the real names
of the men mentioned.

A man is more than the sum of his crimes.
People in prison are unique and yet
they are so ordinary.
Many have committed crimes of a
sickening nature yet some of these very people
show a huge amount of genuine feeling.
I don't know how this can be but
I certainly know it is there.
Life behind bars is a world of its own.

Contents

Foreword

There is a sense of 'us and them' in human relations that pervades all strata of our society. At national level it is always 'them'. They did it; we have to live with it. At local levels the same thing: there is always someone to blame for the situation that allows me to stand outside. This is very true when we look at prisons and those who are inside them. Those inside deserve to be there and it's nothing to do with me, so long as they stay there. I don't want to be involved with them other than to tell them they are wrong. I don't want to have to be there to help 'them' (the prisoners) make amends. That is the job of 'them' (the chaplains)!

And chaplains too can be caught up in the 'caring us' and 'them cared for'. The temptation is there to think or say: I am here to help you, I am the one giving, and you are the one taking. 'Us and them', rather than 'both and'. We can both enable each other: we can both receive and both give when justice is not solely retributive, but restorative as well. 'I am here to walk with you.' I remember well, learning that lesson when I was attending a prison as RC Chaplain. Each weekend when I went into the prison to say

Mass, I used to think it was my force of personality that got the lads to stand up in the mess hall and leave the TV for the Chapel. But I soon realised that the number of lads attending Mass did not depend on me so much as on one of their own. When there was a Catholic lad in prison who had some habit of practice the numbers attending always went up. When that lad finished his sentence and was released, the number at Mass went down. The proclaimer of the Gospel in the prison was not so much me, the Chaplain, as the prisoner. His example was encouraging others to choose to respond. I was not the only channel of God's grace to help them: they were there also to help me – part of the mystery of God's love. Each of us is brother and sister: each of us is our brother's, sister's, keeper. No 'us' and 'them' We are one. We enable each other to reflect the image and likeness of God.

How many times in the Gospel stories are lawyers and priests and authority figures confounded when in answer to their serious questions, Jesus responds with a simple parable that at first sight appears to avoid answering the question. Only on reflection do we become aware that this simple answer has in fact opened up and broadened the debate way beyond their comprehension. Sr Carmel's book reflects this aspect of prison life with its simple stories that are telling examples of the interaction between prisoners, families, prison officers and chaplains: at best, each in their own ways opening up to God through the ministry of the others. It reflects, in the mundane and monotonous routine of prison life, the mystery and excitement of meeting God the healer who restores all things and people. Restorative justice begins in an awareness of the innate goodness of others, even when that goodness is not immediately seen. This little book expresses very simply what one person has seen in daily prison life when they begin from the premise that we are all created in the image and likeness of God. Enjoy it, and reflect on it.

+Terence J. Brain, Bishop of Salford

Introduction

I've thoroughly enjoyed writing this book and reliving the many happy memories the writing of it evoked. Ever since the beginning of my involvement in prison ministry I've always yearned to share with others the good and rewarding experience it is, despite the hardship, the sadness and the frustration which it entails at times. The older I get the more I find that happiness and sadness are often to be experienced side by side.

I began to think about this book when I went to look after my dad in Cork during the last few months of his life. Although it gave me some time for planning, my thoughts and energies were otherwise engaged and I found myself without the time or inclination to turn my mind to serious writing. I chatted with dad about it on occasions and he was always most encouraging. I'm sure he's been looking down from Heaven on me as I wrote it. Family, neighbours and friends in Cork were also very supportive during my time in that beautiful city.

On my return to Wakefield Prison other priorities took over, leaving me little time to concentrate on writing. However, some time ago when I went on my annual retreat to the Jesuit Spirituality Centre in Loyola Hall near Liverpool my thoughts about writing this book surfaced again. I discussed the matter with Fr Gerry O'Mahony SJ, my prayer guide, who himself has written many books. His advice to me was to make the writing of the book a hobby at which I would spend a little time each week. Now, that seemed an achievable goal and I soon got started. An old friend and former teaching colleague, Shelagh Bartley, gave me a lot of practical advice as well as liberal dollops of encouragement. It was to Shelagh I sent a copy of each section of my handwritten work as it emerged and she in turn passed it on to her sister Lucy who typed it up. My grateful thanks to them. I would like to thank the Governor, David Shaw, for allowing me to write about Wakefield. I would like to thank Ian, a life sentence prisoner, who kept me focused on my task. I would also like to thank another kind prisoner, Alan, who suggested to me the title which I've finally selected. As can be seen, I owe most of this book to the contributions made by the prisoners themselves. There are, however, stories which have been deliberately omitted because of very personal memories, and there are stories which I would have loved to include but because the men involved were such high-profile prisoners it has not been possible to share these experiences without the risk of them being identified. I would like to say a special thank you too to my religious Community, to the chaplaincy, and to many other people too numerous to mention who have helped me tell my story. May God bless you all.

1

Reality and Roots

IT was my first day in Wakefield as part of the chaplaincy team. I felt a strange mixture of confidence and nervousness. Using my newly acquired keys for the first time I opened the gate into A Wing and locked it carefully behind me. Two young prisoners eyed me – trying to sum me up, I expect. I smiled and, feeling somewhat embarrassed to be carrying the symbols of captivity, said, "These keys really are a pain." One of them wryly replied, "Give 'em to us Sister and we'll look after them for you." Two minutes later I encountered Kieran who beckoned me towards him with his finger and said, "There are some funny people in this place but take no notice. You'll be alright – I'll look after you." I later learned that Kieran was serving about four life sentences. We had a great chat and it was the first of many chats with many interesting people. I felt I had really arrived at HMP Wakefield.

It was in the early 60s when I was still in training to be a fully fledged Sister of Mercy that my novice mistress Sr Madeleine introduced me to prison and ever since I have felt eternally grateful to her. (I once told this to a prisoner and he said he'd never forgiven the person who first introduced him to prison.) Madeleine had befriended a young Irish lad who subsequently found himself in Armley Prison, Leeds, and as she was about the only friend he had at the time he asked her to visit him there. She considered that it would be good pastoral experience for me to accompany her and how right she was! I went on to become a high school History teacher, a ministry I enjoyed very much. However, I regularly spent many a happy Sunday visiting Wakefield Prison during those years and if some of my pupils don't remember much of the history I taught them I think they may remember some of my prison stories. In 1988 I became a member of our Sisters' leadership team. I found it increasingly difficult to continue to be Head of History while at the same time taking on the fairly considerable amount of travel I was required to do in my new role. Thus I found myself part of the Wakefield Ecumenical Chaplaincy team on 11 September 1989 – a very happy day for me and one I have never regretted. How lucky I was to find myself ministering alongside Barrie Cummins the Catholic chaplain and William Noblett the Anglican chaplain, both deeply committed and of real sterling pastoral stature. God has been very good to me.

2

The Bus Stop

It's a great joy for me just to stand at the bus stop in Hunslet Road, Leeds, at 7.05am. Through all the changing seasons of the year I view the area across the road from that vantage point and even in the depth of winter there's always some green to be seen. It reminds me that there's always hope. Sometimes I have to dash for the bus and sometimes I miss it. Recently when I was still some distance away the lone passenger at the bus stop stopped the bus for me though she herself wasn't getting on that particular one. Having thanked her and still smiling gratefully I said to the bus driver as I offered him my fare, "Isn't it lovely to have friends." His reply was, "Didn't you know I wouldn't have gone without you anyway?" On another occasion when I was about to alight from the silent bus – the journey at that hour of the morning tends to be one when most of the passengers are silent – the driver said in a big loud voice, "Cheerio Carmel, flower. See you soon, love." I can't imagine what those people thought, seeing a veil-clad woman depart with such a greeting, but it certainly put a smile on my face for the rest of the day. These little encounters are little blessings – maybe even big ones in my life.

Incidentally wearing a veil can make a difference in people's perception of a person. I notice that the seat beside me on the bus usually tends to be the last one filled. One morning there were just two empty seats, one beside a black man, and the other beside me. Then there was just one empty seat – the one beside me. I wonder if people thought I was going to question them on their moral lives – and at that hour of the morning too!

On my arrival at the prison one cold, wet wintry morning, a prisoner said, "Hello Sister, how are you?" My reply was, "I stood at the bus stop for half an hour and I was just drenched to the skin and frozen to the marrow." I will never forget his remark, "What wouldn't I give to be standing at a bus stop for half an hour – drenched to the skin and frozen to the marrow." It certainly taught me a salutary lesson. I remember too on that same morning watching a young prisoner emptying dustbins and saying to him, "Paul, what are you doing in your shirtsleeves? Where's your jumper and your jacket? You'll freeze to death." His reply was, "I wish I did." That gave me food for thought all day long and indeed it came to my mind on more than one occasion later. This same Paul later went to London with his brother on an appeal and both were released. I hope and pray they are both happy now.

To come back to the bus stop. Many people have said to me that I should direct my efforts towards helping the victims rather than the offenders. Now I would never like it to be thought that I ignore the victims. My special time of prayer for them is at the bus stop, and goodness knows I spend quite a lot of time at bus stops. Also, if I just happen to miss a bus then that means I have yet more opportunity to pray for victims. An added advantage of this is that it helps me even in a small way to empathise with the prisoners. Indeed I consider it a very minor frustration compared with those which have to be endured by the men in Wakefield Prison.

3
Wakefield Prison

Wakefield is a maximum security prison, housing about 600 prisoners, some of whom are among the most disturbed and disruptive in the system. It has more lifers than any other prison in Western Europe.

There are many buildings within the prison – living accommodation (three main wings radiating from the centre which is the hub of the establishment), workshops, administration, probation and psychology areas, chaplaincy, gym and weights room, healthcare centre, segregation unit, works department, laundry, and education department. Then there's the football pitch and of course the exercise yard so we tend to get plenty of exercise as we go about our duties during the day.

I often pass by the mulberry bush as indeed the prisoners do. This is the original mulberry bush of nursery rhyme fame ("Here we go round the mulberry bush"). It dates back to the time when Wakefield was a women's prison and while the mothers were engaged in their duties the children entertained themselves playing round this tree. At present the prisoners write and publish their own magazine (and kindly allow us to make a contribution) and this publication is called *The Mulberry Bush*.

My daily routines vary. The following could be a typical day. After attending 7.45am Mass at nearby St Austin's church I arrive at the gate of the prison and go through the searching procedure. If one particular officer is on duty he tells me he is "blessing me twice" because as I stand there with outstretched arms he moves his wand in the form of a cross and repeats this when I turn round. He says that by doing this he is "returning the compliment". It's a lovely thought and reminds me so often that even in the most unlikely ways we can be a blessing for each other. I then go to the Administration Department to pick up any messages and from there walk down to the Chaplaincy Department where I'll have a little chat (or maybe a longer one) and a cuppa with the other chaplains. From there I go to the Healthcare Centre and see all the prisoner patients. This is one of our statutory duties as chaplains. If someone is particularly ill or depressed or has some other problem – perhaps thinking about going on a hunger strike – then I'd spend more time with him. They're very kind in the Healthcare Centre, giving me cups of coffee. Some days I feel awash with coffee but I consider it a great kindness on the part of the prisoners to share their very precious coffee with me. There is so often a courtesy and a kindness about prisoners that never fails to impress me. I often notice when we meet at a gate or a door how they will stand back and let me through and I always compliment them on their gentlemanly behaviour, which usually produces a broad smile.

Following this visit I may have to interview a prisoner with a view to writing a report. This is not a part of the work that I particularly like as it sometimes entails reading the records and asking in-depth questions regarding the man's offence. Hopefully though, at the end of the day it will help his progress through the system. When I first started at Wakefield I decided I would "be nice" to these men all the time. As time went on, however, I decided that if I really wanted to help them I would have to challenge them and this I did for some time. However, as I became even more experienced, I saw that the men were constantly being challenged by many people and I concluded that they didn't need me to do this too. Nowadays sometimes I challenge, sometimes I don't, depending on how I assess the situation and how things are with the prisoner. Who knows how I'll approach things tomorrow? I try to go around constantly with my eyes and ears open and more particularly I try to keep my mind and heart open.

At lunchtime I go on to the wings as the men are coming in from the workshops and queueing up for their lunch. One of the best bits of advice I was ever given was to practise "loitering with intent" – that is, just standing about. This I must say was very difficult for me at first, having been a teacher and always busy – as teachers are! What it means is that I do not give the impression of being in any hurry. If a man wants to come along to say "hello" as he passes by with his tray on his way to eat his meal in his cell he can pause for a longer chat if he wants to. There have been many, many occasions when casual chat about the weather has led to much deeper conversations at a later stage. I remember one such occasion when an opening comment on the weather led to a man telling me that his girlfriend who was visiting him that afternoon had just been diagnosed as having cancer.

He feared he might never see her again after that visit. We had a good chat and I was able to see them both in the Visits Area that afternoon.

Following lunch the men are locked in their cells for over an hour. I well remember my first week in Wakefield. Each night when I went to bed I could hear in my head the banging and clanging and locking of the cell doors. I found it awesome and reflected that as far as I knew people didn't even lock up their dogs in the middle of the day. I have since found out that some, but by no means all, of the men are pleased about this as it gives them an opportunity for a siesta – a privilege not available to most of the rest of us.

During lock-up time I have my sandwich and catch up on correspondence and phone calls. I may get in touch with some prison visitors or some family members of a prisoner, especially if someone is ill and the prisoner's phone card has run out. Once a week, unless otherwise engaged, for example by a chaplaincy team meeting (we work as an ecumenical team), I go to an aerobics class in the prison gym, run by Fiona, a prison officer. Other members have included prison officers, psychologists, probation officers, teachers, other chaplains, governors and admin staff, and we manage a little bit of chat in between our rigorous routines. Even though I'd never get the star prize I thoroughly enjoy it.

In the afternoon there may be a meeting to attend, for example, suicide prevention or drugs awareness. Such meetings are usually multi-disciplinary, a good way of working in prison as none of us has the monopoly on the right angle, but together hopefully we can get a better vision of the best way forward. This may be followed by a brief trip to the Visits' Area. Much as I'd love to spend a lot of time there chatting with the men and their visitors I resist the temptation to do so. The reason for this is that visitors have come to see family or friends in the prison. Visiting time is very precious indeed and the time is usually too short. It lifts my heart to see how most of the men have made a special effort to look particularly smart – a measure of how much the visit means to them. One group of visitors that I have a very soft spot for is mothers. I may be accused of being sexist and some people would argue this point but here I merely state what my own experience is. Mothers are the ones who still come along even when everyone else, including dads, have given up. On really bad days, and by that I mean bad weather days or times when prisoners for their own reasons are not very communicative with their families, it is the mothers who, 99 times out of 100, will turn up and be there for them. However, this in no way minimises my admiration for the rest of the family, girlfriends and friends who visit. Prison visitors are volunteers who come to visit men who perhaps are too far from home for their families to travel or who have not yet arrived at a point where they feel able to face family and friends. Perhaps they just wish to see a friendly face from the outside. These men and women to my mind are the salt of the earth. Some of our Sisters visit also and whenever Sr Maria comes in and starts discussing football with the men and telling them about her visits to Elland Road, home of Leeds United Fooball Club, I know I'll definitely have to take a back seat. Such visitors are greatly valued. Visits are a real lifeline and a nice cup of tea and refresh-ments are provided by the WRVS (Women's Royal Voluntary Service). The children are not forgotten either – there is a very alive and active playgroup in one corner of the visits area. On more than one occasion I have seen the great joy on a man's face as on the way back to the wing from visits he proudly shows me the picture drawn or painted for him by his child or niece or nephew. Despite the presence of prison officers around the area, cameras in operation, and the delays sometimes caused by searching procedures too, I think the time spent on visits is a very special and precious time indeed for the men.

I may go from here to the Segregation Unit, or the Block as we generally call it. This visit too is a statutory duty where each day a chaplain is required to see each of the prisoners here. It's always good to see each of those men even if there is usually only time for a smile and a quick hello as the escorting officers take me round the Block. When I arrive there I relinquish my keys (I suppose I'm less valuable as a potential hostage without keys than with them!). If anyone wants a longer conversation or if someone looks particularly depressed or if an officer tells me of a prisoner with a particular need, then I'll come along later for a more in-depth chat. I always say "God bless" to each of them as I leave and on more than one occasion I've been surprised and delighted when I heard a response, "And God bless you too." I've been very lucky in that I have never in all my years come across a prisoner who hasn't spoken to me. I have never met a prisoner who has not had some good in him though it may be a little hard to find at times. In fact I'd say most prisoners despite their offences have more good in them than they or anyone else could imagine. The same is probably true of the rest of us too, despite our offences, whatever our background.

At the end of the day I go home in the No. 110 bus again – usually very tired and weary. The funny thing is that I may be full of negative feelings – sadness, disappointment, frustration, anger at some injustice – and yet I am so grateful to God for letting me walk beside these men.

4

Healing

Dostoevsky said that the degree of civilisation in a society can be judged by entering its prisons. I think about that often and still haven't come to any strong conclusions about the degree of truth in the statement. A lot of evil can be found in prison, a lot of cruelty, injustice, lots of evidence of man's inhumanity to man. I've seen many examples. However, I think that on the whole prisoners underestimate themselves. They have within themselves the power and the force and the ability to help and to heal and to try to make amends even if it can only be in a small way. A lot of healing needs to be done in an atmosphere where there is so much hurt and hatred and bitterness and negativity about.

One of the spectacular ways in which the men show their willingness to "pay back" is in the yearly sponsored half-marathon where the proceeds go to some charity, usually a local one such as Wakefield Hospice. The half-marathon consists of about 84 laps of the football pitch and I think they're heroic to do that. They are usually joined by some members of staff too – though I confess I've never been among the runners (I didn't want to show them up!). I like to cheer them on and am very glad of the opportunity to have a chat with spectators – prisoners and officers. It's usually quite a festive occasion too as those who want to can come out and cheer (and hopefully will have sponsored) the runners. Some even bring their flasks with them. On the last half-marathon one of the men shared his very sweet tea with me. Now, sweet tea is not my favourite drink but the gesture was greatly appreciated.

On the previous day I had been in the Healthcare Centre when one of the men, Joe, brought me coffee, and in a lovely clean mug too. As he handed it to me he said, "Oh dear, there's a hair in it but I'll let you pull it out yourself. I wonder whose it is? At least you can see it's not mine." Joe is bald. Later I was telling another man, Michael, who was in the segregation unit and considered very dangerous, about the half-marathon. His comment was, "Well, I've never been one for running a half-marathon, apart from the times I've been running from the police!"

Prisoners feel they can "pay back" a little by making goods which can be sold or raffled for charity and many have discovered wonderful skills and talents in painting, furniture-making and craft work of all descriptions. It really is a treat to see these men, especially in No. 8 Workshop where goods are made for charity. It's good to see the joy and pride on the men's faces as they are able to use their creative skills. Many have said to me that they know they can never make up for what they have done and the suffering they have caused, but they feel so pleased to be able to make this small contribution.

I consider that the Braille Unit provides an out-standing opportunity of doing something really constructive for the blind. Even after my many years visiting there, the technique is still a big mystery to me but I get great pleasure in seeing how much the men are able to help blind people of all kinds, especially students. I am always fascinated by their ingenuity in making diagrams and am often rather amused to find someone like a fundamentalist Protestant deeply engrossed in his work on Our Lady, Mother of God. On one occasion a man was Brailling night prayers for a Poor Clare Sister who had lost her sight. He expressed great concern that she would not be able to examine her conscience each night because I had not included a specific Examination of Conscience in the book I'd given him. I found it very interesting that a man in a maximum security prison should be so concerned about the spiritual welfare of a contemplative nun. It's lovely to think of the different ways in which we look after each other. Thinking of the Braille Unit reminds me of a young man named Paul who worked there. He was particularly talkative and was somewhat of a dis-traction to the other men until someone lighted on the wonderful idea of getting Paul to do a sponsored silence. Being a friendly and obliging fellow by nature he agreed and I was asked to select the charity so I chose Victim Support. He did very well and there was satisfaction all around when I proudly brought the considerable amount of money he had collected to the Wakefield Victim Support office which on that occasion was manned by a retired prison officer. I'll speak more of prison officers later but I am constantly being surprised by the amount of good work done by many of them for charities.

I am constantly being surprised too by the generos-ity shown by some prisoners with their very limited amount of money. In the days when such "gestures" were allowed one man called Tony spent a very considerable amount of his money in the weeks before Christmas buying bars of chocolate from the canteen which he sent to a school where there were a lot of poor children. I will always have the memory of Tony's big smile each year as he told me the chocolate bars were ready to be collected. I think the joy that he got from giving was even greater than the joy the children got from receiving.

That gesture brings to my mind John, also doing a life sentence and a man of great generosity. Some years ago, when he was earning £16.00 a month, he donated £12.00 of this sum towards the education of a little girl, Lolita, in the Philippines (organised by an agency in London). John loved to smoke tobacco but this was a habit he had to give up, something he did willingly so that Lolita could be educated. Here was a man who always had a big smile too as he showed me Lolita's progress reports sent from London.

On many occasions I have said that the best help any man in Wakefield Prison can get, generally speaking, is that provided by another man in Wakefield Prison. The rest of us may help him in many ways but at the end of the day we go home so how can we really feel what it is like to be a prisoner? To my mind, the ministry of "like-to-like" is very important – in any walk of life but particularly in a place like Wakefield Prison.

So often, the healing is in the telling for all of us and as a rule we feel so much better when we have been able to tell our story and feel that it has been heard. A very successful "Listeners" scheme exists in the prison. Volunteer prisoners are given basic training in listening skills (as well as basic first-aid and so on) and this enables them to provide what I consider to be an excellent service. It is great that this service is recognised by prison staff. Sometimes when a man has difficulties it may not be easy for him to approach a chaplain or another member of staff but it may not be a problem for him to approach another prisoner, feeling that here is someone who will really understand what he is going through. I have seen prisoners who have been greatly helped by such encounters and I have known of occasions when men have worked through their suicidal thoughts and been brought to a more positive outlook through the help of a "listener". I have heard these men described by their peers as kind, caring, helpful and capable and I have felt humbled sometimes by their thought for each other. My mind goes back to some years ago when the scheme first started. Joe's mother died unexpectedly and he was devastated by the news. One man gave him his phone card so that he could have more contact with home. Another man gave him a tape of Daniel O'Donnell who had been his mother's favourite singer. Yet another man gave him batteries so that he could use his tape recorder (Joe was not very organised regarding how he spent his money). When Joe woke up the morning following the news of his mother's death, he found a mug of tea on the locker beside his bed. He never found out who put it there!

I think of Bill, unable to read or write but desperately anxious to keep contact with his children, and the many hours that Phil spent with him until he had mastered the art to some degree. Bill was able to use the facilities provided in the Education Department but it was the teaching skills of Phil that touched him because he knew that Phil understood from experience the difficulties of keeping strong family ties while in prison.

I well remember the day that Julian left the Health-care Centre to spend the remainder of his days in the nearby hospice. I stood with him as he said goodbye to Reg. Tears were in the eyes of both of them – and mine too – as he thanked Reg for the way in which he had helped him during those last difficult days when he was able to do so little for himself. I was so happy to see Julian in the hospice – in those beautiful surroundings where he was also surrounded by the love of his family. I have always been pleased to see men who are terminally ill being able to go to the hospice but I have always been saddened when local papers or radio stations have given advance publicity calling them dreadful names and in a way criticising the hospice for taking them in. The hospice responds to people according to their needs and I have always felt so proud and so grateful to Wakefield Hospice because they have had the courage and the good heart to look after our men in their hour of need. To a certain extent, I suppose, I understand the negative attitude of members of the public. There are men in Wakefield Prison who have done extremely violent deeds and there are men in Wakefield Prison still capable of doing extremely violent deeds. I have seen instances of this and it is not a pretty sight. I remember once visiting a man who had had part of his ear bitten off. I nearly fainted. He saw this and promptly sat at the other side of me so that I was facing his good ear! I shall never forget seeing one of our probation officers a few minutes after she had been violently attacked. Later I even summed up courage to tell the man responsible what I thought of him and his actions. However, hand in hand with this situation there is a good side and I certainly encounter this good side much more than the bad and evil side.

Yes, prisoners try to make restitution to society by endeavouring to pay back even in a small way. Many of them also find a channel of repentance in helping each other – something which I've seen come naturally to many. Many prisoners have also helped me personally and I have often felt that I receive far more than I could ever give to them. Now I don't want to suggest that all is always sweetness and light in my relationships with them. We all have our moments. On one occasion when I visited a man in the Segregation Unit he shouted out to the officers, "Don't bring that old battleaxe near me." Well I was a bit taken aback. It was a blow to be called a battleaxe but to be called an *old* battleaxe was a bitter pill to swallow!

My experience of the men in Wakefield on the whole is that they are kind and gentleman-like to me. On one occasion when I thanked a man for being so courteous to me he said, "They've taken just about everything away from me but they can't take away my manners." There's a ready smile which I greatly appreciate. At some point of most days I'm told a joke which usually puts a smile on my face. Recently a very serious young man, John, told me about the fellow who was stopped by the police for speeding. He explained that he was only doing what the notice on his driving licence told him to do. The policeman was very curious and asked him what this was. The fellow confidently produced his piece of paper, pointing out to the policeman the words: '*Tear along the dotted line*'.

There have been times when I felt particularly that I was the person being ministered to by the prisoners. Three such occasions spring readily to mind.

One day we had a particular difficulty with a member of the chaplaincy team who had got himself into the *Sun* newspaper. This was a cause of great sadness indeed and I had to endure more than one snide remark in the prison, but not from prisoners. On the day following the publication of the article David, a prisoner, asked if he could have a word with me. I assumed he wanted to discuss some problem he had but instead he said he wanted to hear how I was. He wanted to let me know that he was praying particularly for me and for the chaplaincy and that a number of the men were praying specially at this time. "It's only fair" he said. "You help us when we need it – and now we are doing the same for you."

The second occasion where I felt particularly supported was when I was in hospital with a serious illness. As a rule I don't keep letters but the ones which I received from prisoners were ones which I held on to for a very long time because they were so full of caring, understanding and affection. It amazed me to find how many people were praying for me and I was particularly touched when men would write something like, "Well, as you know, I'm not sure I believe in God but I asked him if he really existed to look after you." I even received gifts which were so, so special to me. One man wrote to say he'd looked round his cell to see what he could send me which was really, really precious to him and he sent me a postcard of a Vauxhall car which he said was his most prized possession. Another man sent me his well-used copy of Philip Larkin's poetry, hoping it would give me as much pleasure as it had always given him. To this day I am convinced that the love shown at that time contributed as much to my complete recovery as did the surgery and medication. Some might say that those letters and gifts represented a real rogues' gallery. Fr Barnabas Aherne, whom I often listened to as a young Sister, used to compare St Luke's Gospel to a rogues' gallery, and I think the men in Wakefield sometimes seem to come straight from the pages of the Gospel.

The third occasion on which I felt greatly ministered to by prisoners was on my return to Wakefield after the death of my mother. When I went to the Segregation Unit the four prisoners who were cleaners there invited me to join them for coffee in their little room. The five of us sat down round the table with our drinks and one man, John, produced a bar of KitKat which he had bought for me after hearing of the death of my mother. They then asked me to tell my story of the events surrounding my last trip home. I told my story and for me the healing was in the telling; it was certainly a therapeutic experience for me. All four gave me their full and individual attention and when I had finished one of them, Dave, said, "From what you'd told us about your parents I thought your father would probably die first. I tried to puzzle out why your mother died first and I think I've got the answer. She was always good for looking after your dad so I think she went to Heaven to pick out a little house and get it ready for him. I seem to remember something in the Bible about God having a lot of houses in Heaven." Dave's explanation brought a smile to my face and comfort too. It made me reflect with gratitude that we are all wounded healers and how wonderful it is that we can help each other so much.

5

Religion

A strange and fascinating thing is religion – something I find difficult to define. It has sometimes led to strange happenings. As a student of history it used to fascinate me to discover the number of things that were done in the name of religion. The number of religious wars that took place never ceased to amaze me.

Religion in prison is a strange thing too. I have known men who have lost faith there. I have known men who have become very cynical about religion. I have known men who have become very angry at the memory of things they endured in childhood from people who called themselves religious. In my experience I have not seen very large numbers of men attend chapel apart from special occasions like the Carol Service. However, I would draw a distinction between a man being a religious person and a man being a spiritual person. My experience is that many men do not attend chapel services, yet they are spiritual and often draw huge comfort from this. Their prayers may not be of the conventional type but very much individual and from the heart, and for that reason I feel they are all the more genuine. One man, Neil, once said to me, "I'm fed up to the teeth with this God business. Church doesn't work for me because when I come back to the wing I start swearing all over again." We chatted about it and I discovered that Neil talked to God in his own words each night before he went to bed. Now isn't that a fine prayer?

Fred approached me one day and asked, "Could you teach me how to pray?" I said, "Of course I can," and later that day we had a great chat. Fred told me he'd never prayed, but the previous night he was thinking a lot about his offence and about the pain and sadness he had inflicted on others. He wanted to tell God he was sorry but he said he didn't know how to go about doing that. In the end he just said, "God, I'm sorry," and as he uttered those words the tears began to fall and he wept and wept for a long time. Now if that isn't prayer I wonder what is? We had many a talk after that and I would consider that Fred is a man very close to God.

Colin stopped me on the landing one day and said, "I'd like to be baptised. Could you tell me what to do?" In our chat later on that day he told me that he had been abandoned by his mother and abused by his foster-father. He eventually ran away from his foster home and amazingly was able to track down his mother, but she still didn't want to know him. "Now", he said "I'm 25 and at the beginning of a life sentence. I feel I've been let down by people all my life and I thought that if I turned to Jesus he wouldn't let me down but would look after me." I think perhaps it was the prayers of some good person out there in the world – maybe somebody who was suffering themselves – which were responsible for Colin taking that first step in faith. Although the way is still hard for him, it is much more bearable with Jesus at his side. Yes, faith can sustain and be very real, and as Gerry O'Mahony says in his book *Simply Free*, "If I am aware of being God's child I can hold my head up anywhere." There is hope for Colin.

I well remember being very inspired by a group of men soon after my arrival at Wakefield. These men had formed a rosary group and would recite the rosary in twos or threes whenever possible, using each other's cells. One day six Jesuit priests and two others were murdered in El Salvador. That night each member of the rosary group knelt down by his bed at 9.00pm (they had been locked up at 8.00pm). They said the rosary for those who had been murdered and for the people who were responsible for this dreadful act. However, I must keep the record straight. Danny was the leader of this group and I have to admit that his zeal on occasion was a little excessive. When he failed to extract a promise from me that I would say the rosary at a specific time each night, he threatened to write a letter of complaint to the principal Roman Catholic Chaplain and to my Mother Superior! Devotion to Mary our mother has greatly helped some of the men. This puts me in mind of Ged with whom I've had many a chat about religion. Ged confided in me that although he had great love for God he had great difficulty in relating to him as a father, because of the extremely difficult relationship he had had with his own father. On the other hand, he got on very well indeed with his mother and if there was something he particularly wanted of his father he would ask his mother to put in a good word for him. Because of this personal experience, Ged found it much easier to pray to Mary and to ask her to intercede for him with God. "Do you think God minds if I give so much attention to Our Lady?" he asked. What a depth of prayer!

Thinking of Ged brings to mind my second encounter with him, when the custody of his children was to be decided by the courts. He was to be taken out to the court hearing and he was full of anxiety as to the outcome. He specially requested that I would be there in the prison on his return and I thanked God that I was able to do this for him. I thanked God too for the flexibility in our religious duties in Community which enabled me to be there for him when he needed me.

Prayer to Our Lady is popular with some of the men. I suppose this is very understandable as mothers are such an important part of their lives. Mothers are their rock, their foundation, their stability – fragile though it all may be. One man, Lee, once said to me that although he hadn't seen or heard from his mother for about four years she was still his driving force. I found that hard to work out but then I still find a lot of things hard to work out. The happy thing is that I don't have to work it all out. We see the stars, we don't have to work out how they get there for us to enjoy them. To come back to Our Lady. A man called Keith once asked me for a picture of Our Lady for his cell. Keith was doing several life sentences for some horrendous offences and I was somewhat surprised by this request. He said that Mary had a calming influence on his soul and on the turmoil which was constantly with him. Looking at her picture always brought him some peace, which he found to be a very rare commodity in his life. I hope and pray she continues to keep him under her protection. He certainly needs it.

It causes me distress to think about the lack of

peace in prison. There are so many tortured souls. Granted, some of these have robbed others of their peace and a lot of their mental torture is caused by a guilty conscience calling out to be heard. Some suffer terrible dreams and are frightened to go to sleep at night. On more than one occasion I have chatted with officers who tell me their experiences of night duty and how they can hear prisoners crying out in their sleep or even crying out in despair in their sleeplessness. I recall Alan in the Segregation Unit who did his utmost every night to keep awake as long as possible. He said that each night after he had gone to sleep the ghost of his son, who had died aged 12 in a road accident, would waken him and look reproachfully at him. Because of what had happened in Alan's own life he was unable to grieve for his son until many years afterwards and this grief left him in the depths of despair. We had many a chat and I still keep him in my prayers.

Some prisoners have a strong sense of evil and its power. I remember many years ago, being summoned to visit Ken in the Segregation Unit. Ken was extremely agitated and felt the devil was in the cell with him. He had requested that water be placed around him for protection. The officers had done this in their attempts to bring him peace. He was still extremely agitated when I arrived but I definitely had no feeling of the presence of an evil spirit. I have never in all my time in Wakefield felt the presence of an evil spirit.

I asked myself the question, "What is the predominant feeling here?" I concluded it was fear or even terror on the part of Ken. I then crossed the line over the screen of water, put my arm around him and said, "Ken, God is stronger than the devil. We'll say a little prayer together." We prayed together the Lord's Prayer. I don't know how much peace it brought to Ken but he certainly seemed calmed and when I last saw him he was a man much more at peace with himself.

The Lord's Prayer is a prayer I have often recited with prisoners, first because I think it's the greatest prayer of all and secondly because it is familiar to just about everyone brought up in the Christian tradition, however tenuous their links with it. I well remember visiting Tony in the Healthcare Centre. Because he was so disturbed at the time I was not allowed into his cell nor was I allowed to speak to him through an open door. Our conversation took place from opposite sides of a locked door. Tony asked me to pray for him, which I did. I then suggested the Lord's Prayer which we recited together from our respective positions, standing at either side of the cell door. I wondered what staff made of this form of ministry but at least there were no snide comments made to Tony – in my hearing anyway.

Speaking of a locked door reminds me of a video we once showed of the Profession of a Poor Clare Sister, Sr Pia Francis, who with other members of her community in York corresponded with some of the men in Wakefield. The men were fascinated by the video of the Sisters whose lifestyle in so many ways resembled their own. One of the men, Clive, asked if the Sisters were locked up in their cells at night! I think it is absolutely wonderful that people like these pray for each other. I once gave a talk on religious life. At the end of it, one of the men, Ron, said, "I really enjoyed that talk." I mentally gave myself a pat on the back but that was short-lived as Ron went on to say, "If I have to do time for the crime I've committed, I'm glad I can do it in a prison and not in a convent." It came as quite a shock to me to realise I'd painted such a picture. Incidentally, I'm sure I could not minister so happily in prison if I did not have the love and support I experience in my Community life.

It is my privilege sometimes to bring Communion to men in the Segregation Unit who request it. Though these are men who are usually in this unit because of misbehaviour in the main part of the prison, I have experienced a sensitivity to the receiving of Communion which I have never found elsewhere. When I came to his cell, Kevin's eyes would light up and he would say with great eagerness, "Have you brought Jesus to me?" Then there was Dominic. To say he was not an angel would be – shall we say – an understatement, and yet when I brought Communion to him in his cell he showed an awareness and reverence and knowledge and sensitivity of what it was all about that left me very humbled.

Then there was Matthew, for whom receiving Holy Communion had such a calming effect that on each occasion without fail he asked me to pray for his victim. I always feel so happy to be able to minister and hopefully bring some peace into their troubled minds and hearts.

Communion doesn't feature largely in the lives of a lot of the prisoners directly, but it can feature indirectly. I remember James saying to me one Friday afternoon, "Come along on Monday. I'll have something wonderful to show you and I know you'll love it." Well, I'd never win the title "Memory Woman of the Year", so once I was out of sight I made a little note in my note book to see James on Monday. What he had to show me was a beautiful photograph of his daughter's first Communion. What a proud father he was but how sad I felt that he could not be alongside his wife and daughter for that lovely occasion. I always encourage the men to show me family photos and often I'm shown school reports as well. Having been a schoolteacher I'm well experienced in picking up the positive comments and making the most of them.

Thinking of teaching brings to mind a university lecturer, Alan, doing a life sentence. He told me he did not consider himself a religious man but chatting with me one day in late December he confided that the best Christmas he had ever spent was the one we had just had, his first in prison. Normally he would spend the season frantically buying Christmas presents and busying himself with parties, which he convinced himself were a source of real enjoyment for him. However, during this particular Christmas season these activities did not involve him. Instead he had time to reflect and to pray on the real meaning of Christmas and time also to listen to seasonal music on his radio, and this experience brought him a happiness hitherto unknown. That particular Christmas was also marked for me by a touching event. I was contacted by a young teacher, Margaret, in a Catholic primary school in Huddersfield. She was doing a project with her 10-year-olds on caring for others. Some of those children had parents in prison. She wanted to make a positive gesture in that direction and so the children made a beautiful coloured garland in which each link represented a prayer for someone in prison, said by the child who made it. One evening after school she came along to my convent in Hunslet, Leeds, with some of the children. We had a nice little chat, a little party and they gave me the garland which I took into the prison next day and which made a very colourful and meaningful decoration round the altar of the chapel for Christmas Day. The men were very touched and very happy to know those children were praying for them and I was very happy that such a spiritual link had been made. What a blessing people like Margaret are for us all.

Religion is certainly very personal at times. I recall Michael (he whose only marathon was when he ran from the police!) saying that every morning he looks up at the heavens and says, "Just get me through today Gov." Michael is by no means the only one who has used his cell as a little chapel. Arthur once told me that he liked to pray in his cell in the evening when there was a lull in the noise of the prison. At this time of day the evening sun shone through the bars in his window, casting a shadow on his wall which, if you used your imagination, created a stained-glass window effect.

I often reflect on the words of Gerry Hughes in his book *The God of Surprises* where he says that it is in our woundedness and not in our power that we find God. How true. I think too that in a way we all belong to that category so there's still hope for us all.

6

Buckingham Palace

I've always had a soft spot for Princess Anne because of her dedication to duty and her good works. Before I joined the chaplaincy team she visited Wakefield Prison to see the excellent Braille Unit there. I was so delighted that I decided to write and thank her for doing this. However, I was very busy at the time and so the letter was written in the little space between running the bath one night and actually getting into it. I felt more than rewarded by the lovely reply I eventually received.

Imagine how thrilled I was when, a few years ago, I was nominated for a Butler Trust Award. This is the Prison Service annual award scheme. As ever there was prisoner support and I later heard that some of the men, headed by Ian, wrote supporting letters. I received the award at Buckingham Palace and to my delight it was presented by the Princess Royal, Princess Anne.

There was great excitement and needless to say I had plenty of offers from people more than willing to do escort duty for me – prisoners and staff. One tall, handsome officer called Dave still reminds me that I turned him down. Because this was such an important occasion for me I felt that my guest just had to be a family member as my family is my greatest support. I brought my sister Sheila with me as my guest.

The sun shone that day so it was brilliance within and brilliance without – all day long. The Palace was absolutely magnificent and it was like a fairy tale being in there – nothing but splendid luxury all around.

The ceremony took place in the ballroom – scene of the creation of many knights, and the essence of grandeur. What a contrast to Wakefield Prison and how I would have loved to have all those people present who were responsible for me being there. The Princess looked charming in her black skirt and shoes and gloves and yellow jacket. It was lovely to hear her speak so knowledgeably about the prison situation. I was very impressed indeed. At her side stood Lord Woolf, for whom I also had a great admiration because of the efforts he made to make life more humane for those in prison. As I received my award from Lord Woolf, Princess Anne said, "It's obvious you enjoy your work very much." What a perceptive lady! Following the ceremony, group photos were taken in the Minstrels' Gallery. I could hardly believe this was really happening to me.

We then had our delicious buffet lunch, beautifully presented with silver cutlery and linen napkins. The dining room overlooked the picturesque lawn where we could see the corgis exercising. Surprisingly the menu was in French. I would have expected everything in Buckingham Palace to be thoroughly English. We had creamed chicken on a bed of rice and curried lamb on a bed of rice. There was lettuce with diced beetroot on top and lettuce with creamed celery and a sprinkling of very tasty herbs. For dessert we had peaches set in a mousse with fresh cream. There was red and white wine, orange juice and mineral water. We finished off with coffee and cream. What a pity we felt too excited to be really hungry.

Princess Anne spoke to each award winner and guest in the Music Room. Sheila and I had at least five minutes with her. Before I left Wakefield, Jeremy, a prisoner, had given me two beautiful little matchstick crosses to present to her for Peter and Zara. As I gave them to her, her eyes lit up and they were the eyes of a mother, pleased that someone had thought of her children. Our escort from the Butler Trust offered to look after them for her but she declined the offer and with a big smile put them in her own handbag. I was so pleased and grateful that Jeremy had been so thoughtful. Our conversation centred on the prisoners and Princess Anne enquired about craft-making in Wakefield. I told her what a lot was being done and how it helped the prisoners to "make up" in a little way for what they had done. She then spoke about spirituality and felt it would be easier for men to express this in prison. She wondered if their degree of commitment would continue on their release. I was very impressed by her knowledge and understanding. She also spoke to both of us about our family.

Following the meal everybody mingled freely and I was amazed that there was such a relaxed atmosphere in such an august place. I was really pleased to have a little chat with Brendan O'Friel, former Governor of Strangeways Prison in Manchester. Then I chatted with the Hon. James Butler, whose father was responsible for the 1944 Education Act – an act which I had studied in considerable detail and which had impressed me very much as a teacher. We had a great chat. Then I spoke at length with Lord Woolf, and was delighted to be able to thank him personally for all he had tried to do for prisoners. It was really good to meet Terry Waite too, and he certainly influenced my thinking. In Wakefield whenever I met a man on hunger strike I used to try to show him that this was not the way of achieving his objective and that he could possibly succeed by going about it in more acceptable ways. Now when I meet a man on hunger strike I just ask him to tell me his story. It was from Terry Waite that I learned that sometimes a prisoner feels that going on hunger strike is the only way that will make people listen to him. This was Terry's own experience as a hostage. I met many more people there though unfortunately the Home Secretary was unable to attend – I would have loved to have had a word in his ear! The style was very impressive too. I'd even got a new suit for the occasion. I also had a new veil, which had been made for me by a prisoner in Wakefield doing a number of life sentences.

The only little cloud on my horizon that day was knowing that Yorkshire TV would be waiting for me outside the gates of Buckingham Palace, which made me feel very nervous indeed. However, I was pleased to have the opportunity to say that the men in Wakefield are not the beasts that the media some-times make them out to be, but that there is a tremendous amount of good in them if we take the trouble to find it.

Afterwards Sheila and I went to visit Richard and Chris, old family friends, where we had a delicious meal. Also, a wonderful surprise party awaited me when I returned to my Community. How happy I was to share all this good news with the Community. If it wasn't for their continued tolerance and support I doubt I'd have made it to Buckingham Palace. I always enjoy a celebration and I certainly got great mileage out of the event. When I got on the bus on my return to prison some days later the bus driver said that he'd seen me on TV and he was so pleased to be able to boast to his wife that I was one of his passengers.

It was a wonderful privilege indeed to receive the award at Buckingham Palace, but for me it is an even greater privilege to be able to minister in Wakefield Prison.

7

I don't like...

There are quite a few things that irritate me and even at times anger me about prison life.

I don't like the long time people sometimes have to wait before getting in for visits (though staff will sometimes tell me it's unavoidable).

I don't like the "no smoking" rule though I know that makes me politically incorrect. I think there should be a certain little designated area for smoking because I have seen, even in my days as a teacher, what comfort a cigarette can give in a stressful situation.

I don't like it when men are put in prison far away from their family.

I don't like it when prisoners who should be receiving care in a psychiatric establishment (secure if necessary) are on normal location in a prison. It's not fair to themselves or to the other prisoners or to the staff who look after them.

I don't like it when appointments to see prisoners are not kept, or men are told "Leave it with me" when they make a request and so often nothing happens.

I don't like the slowness with which things appear to happen.

I don't like the system of incentives and privileges, a system which in theory appears very reasonable (and occasionally works very well). Too often I have seen a situation where a man who is particularly institutionalised and manipulative can do well for himself, whereas a man who is inadequate – and there are many such men in prison – and therefore in my opinion more needy will not be able to achieve even standard privileges.

I don't like it when prisoners, especially very ill ones, are handcuffed in outside hospitals.

I don't like it when talent is wasted, when initiative is taken away, when the work ethic is ignored, when self-esteem is destroyed.

I don't like the manner in which some convictions are arrived at in court. I sometimes feel that justice depends on a person's point of view. People have sometimes said to me, "If you have any grain of moral integrity in you, how can you remain where you are?" I'm not one for the grand dramatic gesture, especially if I see it as non-productive. A drop in the ocean is good enough for me. I'm so glad I'm not a judge and that I don't have to judge anyone at all.

8

Some Random Thoughts

How do long-term prisoners really think – especially if they are men responsible for the death of another human being? I've often asked myself that question and I still don't know the answer – nor will I ever, simply because as human beings we are all so complex. No matter how well we know another human being there is always the mystery of each other.

Oh yes, there are among the men those who are devious and manipulative and often full of other negative qualities. I have on the odd occasion seen men when they have completely lost control of their temper, and the sight was a fearful one. I have seen men in the depths of despair when they have just made a suicide attempt, and the sight was a heart-rending one. I have seen men with a look of hate in their eyes, and the sight was an awesome one.

As a rule I don't read prisoners' records unless I have a reason to, for example if I'm writing a report on a particular man. Sometimes men have said to me, "I never committed that offence." There are times when that statement may be true. More often, there are times when that statement is not true. This does not always mean that the man is lying. Sometimes the burden of it is so terrible that the mind blocks it out for a time and the man cannot comprehend how he could possibly commit such an offence. I remember in particular one man, Dave, who spent 33 years agonising over the events surrounding the death of his wife before he was able to admit to himself, let alone others, that he was responsible for her death. It sometimes takes years before an awareness of what he has done becomes acceptable to the prisoner. It can be a slow, painful business. Of course some people never come to terms with it despite all the efforts of treatment programmes. On the other hand I have known men who have felt greatly helped in the understanding of their offence by these programmes.

There have been occasions when, in quite long chats with some of the men, they have been somewhat economical with the truth and my efforts to help them have merely resulted in causing me embarrassment. I suppose I'm not too surprised to be taken in on occasion and it doesn't really anger me – if it doesn't happen too often! I sometimes wonder what I'd do or say if I was in the same position myself. Maybe the same! Sometimes too, men tell a story to their families which doesn't always compare with facts. Eventually when they come to terms with their situations and wish to "come clean", telling the family the truth can be a major difficulty for them because of their natural instinct to protect their family's good name and their own good name too. I have met men too who will always justify their own actions and all the logic and evidence in the world won't persuade them that they have done wrong. It's difficult to deal with such men. Drink and drugs and poor family background have a lot to answer for but why else do some men commit horrendous offences? I don't know but I have a little theory which helps me to be able to cope with such people. It's this. Some people are born with physical deficiencies, which in later life may develop into something like cancer or blindness. These are not the fault of the person concerned, rather something that inspires our pity. Similarly I feel that some people are born with – shall we say – psychological deficiencies which in later life may develop into traits which cause them to commit unspeakable offences which are beyond their control. Of course we feel pity for the victims, but somehow we don't feel pity for the people responsible and we punish rather than help them. On one occasion I discussed this theory with a prominent member of our psychology department but she did not find it an acceptable theory. However, I still feel there is some bit of truth in it.

Then there is the question of forgiveness. This is something that the men find very difficult. Some men ignore it completely but often a man will say to me, "I think of my offence every day and all the sorrow it has caused." The story of the Prodigal Son is a favourite one even for those who are not very familiar with Scripture. Often, though, the men will say, "Maybe God forgives me, but I cannot forgive myself." As previously mentioned, a number of the men turn to charity work as part of their attempt to find forgiveness. Each man's conscience is his own. I often think of the words of Jesus: "There is more joy in Heaven over the one sinner who repents than over the ninety-nine who have no need of repentance."

9

A Haven of Refuge

Having got all that off my chest I can now turn to our haven of refuge in the prison – the chapel. For me the chapel is a very special place even though all would not agree with me as to its relative importance. I remember many years ago when I lived in our new convent in Yeadon, just outside Leeds, we had a visit from a group of our local Methodists. We showed them round the convent and at one point I said that the chapel was the most important room in the house. Standing beside me was one of our Sisters, Camillus, a very down-to-earth lady who immediately commented, "Don't believe a word of it. The kitchen is by far the most important place." Well, that set the record straight and put me in my place. However, I still say I love the chapel in Yeadon and I love the chapel in Wakefield too.

When the chapel of the Good Shepherd in the prison was opened some years ago it seemed very bare. It was obvious that we needed to create a "Wakefield" atmosphere – something that we could call our own and something that would reflect some of the talent and skill of our own men. It would be so nice for the men who came to church on Sunday mornings to be able to worship in beautiful surroundings rather than having to look out of the windows at bars and walls and ribbon wire.

I approached Mike, and asked if he would design some stained glass windows. This prisoner was very artistic and also very committed to his faith. The windows show Jesus the Good Shepherd at the centre, and the sheep at his feet, safe and protected. He is standing at the edge of the water and there is a figure coming out of the water which represents each one of us in Wakefield as we look to Jesus for comfort and guidance. As Mike was a Category A prisoner it was with some difficulty that I managed to arrange a meeting in the chapel which included Mike, Barbara and Barry, the stained glass window specialists, Tom, an officer from Risley, and our then Governor, Bob Duncan, who supported us all along the way. I was really impressed by the sharing of ideas at that meeting and the amount of respect and enthusiasm that abounded. Mike's views were particularly noted by the rest of us and acted upon.

The windows were made for us at HMP Risley. Being designed from a prisoner's perspective makes them all the more special. The colour of the windows is most striking – earth colours – green, brown, ochre, which are not often seen in prison. The men can look at the trees and flowers and flowing water and hopefully this will help to bring them peace and to build up a personal relationship with Jesus. The lines are arranged so as to have a wall effect and serve to remind us that though Wakefield Prison is surrounded by high walls, no wall need ever come between God and us. The flowers too are a sign of hope. "Consider the lilies of the field. They don't labour or sow and yet Solomon in all his glory was not arrayed as one of these." If God can do this for the lilies, what can he not do for each of us? There is a little path in the picture and that too is significant. It has no obstructions. In spite of everything that happens in prison, or in life, we can still go straight along this path on our journey to God without real obstructions. There is also a little bridge and this shows the connectedness between God and us. I think that these windows are particularly beautiful when the sun comes shining through during Mass on Sunday mornings – reminding us that we can be better people and more able to help others when we let God's light shine in us.

We also have a lovely cross in the chapel and that has an interesting little story attached to it too. Some of the oak window frames had to be removed prior to the installation of the stained glass windows. Steve spotted these pieces and immediately saw their potential. It wasn't all plain sailing but eventually he was able to make a distinctive cross from the pieces of oak which were destined for the scrapheap. In Steve's own words: "Prisons are full of people whom society has 'scrapped' but in the hands of God, the most skilful craftsman of all, each one can become beautiful again." The wood is naturally grained, has grooves for adornment, and is a unique item. Despite there being millions of wooden crosses in our world, this one is unique. Such too is the uniqueness of each one of us in our maker's eyes.

Rope bindings appear at the very centre of the cross. Even such sturdy material as solid oak needs to be supported in certain circumstances, just as people need God's support.

The bindings on the cross-piece are broken. Jesus' death and resurrection broke the bonds of sin and suffering. The ropes that would have lashed each one of us to our own "cross" are broken. We can all be free in Christ Jesus.

No wonder I often ask myself, "Who is ministering to whom?" We chaplains are indeed privileged to be ministering and to be ministered to in such an environment. However, I have to say that not all our stories are success stories. I had a dream of having a lovely "Wakefield" statue of Our Lady in the chapel. It seemed too as if this dream might come true. The Bishop of Lincoln kindly brought us a big block of oak from Lincoln Cathedral. It was about 500 years old and I felt it would be deeply steeped in the prayer of all those centuries. To help Tony, who had volunteered to carve the statue, I brought into the prison the convent statue of Our Lady from its pedestal in our chapel. Some time later a visitor to our convent chapel asked where Our Lady was and you can imagine her surprise on hearing the reply, "Oh she's behind bars in Wakefield Prison." Tony was very keen to try his hand but alas – instead of us seeing the effects of the wood being full of prayer we soon became aware of effects of a much more earthly quality. It was full of cracks and was as hard as rock. Some time later Tony moved to another prison so who knows what the future holds. I'm sure that one day we will have an inspiring statue of Our Lady.

Objects can inspire us but people can inspire us even more. If I were asked, "Who, of all the people you have met, has in your opinion done most to help prisoners and their families?" my answer would be Sr Annunciata from Portsmouth. She had been a teacher in a private school but changed her ministry so that she could follow more closely the church's option for the materially poor. Her area of work in

Portsmouth included Kingston Prison. In the days before hospice care was generally available she obtained permission on more than one occasion to bring a terminally ill prisoner to her home so that the Sisters could look after him and he could die somewhere other than in prison. On my first visit to Sr Annunciata's house I had to sleep in the chapel because she had already given the only spare room to a poor Liverpool family who had come down to see their son in prison. On another occasion, I stayed at their little farm which at that time employed about six needy men. I was instructed by Annunciata to speak to each of them and to compliment them on the good work they were doing. In the prison she really cared about the prisoners and she really cared about the staff too. She was a woman of independent mind but a very large heart. Folk like her are the salt of the earth – a real inspiration.

10
Church Services

Many of our encounters with God happen in unlikely places and in the presence of apparently unlikely people. It's hard at times to see God in each other. On one occasion a man called Colin told me how wrong I was to believe that Jesus Christ was God. He gave me a long lecture on this topic. My feet were aching but I felt it would be churlish not to let him have his say. He then advised me to go off and reflect on what he had told me so that I would soon come to realise the error of my beliefs. On another occasion Kevin told me a chaplain had given him a copy of St Luke's Gospel. He said it was only later he realised it was a Catholic version and so he put it down the toilet. He also told me the only really worthwhile Gospel was St Mark's, but I have to confess that I didn't pursue the subject and ask for his reasons for making that statement. It would have been interesting.

I have been and am always pleased to see the men in chapel – well, with one exception perhaps, and that was Henry. Henry was reported to have tried to set fire to 47 churches so I was perhaps just a little bit nervous in case he showed interest in coming along.

I needn't have worried as that was one area of the prison which he religiously avoided. Weren't we lucky!

If a close member of a prisoner's family dies, the prisoner is generally allowed to go to the funeral. There might be difficulty in getting permission for this if the prisoner was a very violent man, or if he had a history of trying to escape or if the family had very strong reasons to want him to remain away. If a man was not allowed to go to the funeral of a relative or close friend then he would sometimes come along to the chapel – usually at the time that coincided with the funeral service. On these occasions, or on anniversaries, one of the chaplaincy team would say prayers with the prisoner and chat with him about his thoughts and feelings regarding the dead person. After my first such experience I always made sure to bring a box of tissues into the chapel. Its amazing what a depth of sensitivity, remorse and genuine goodness such an occasion often reveals.

We've had some lovely services in the chapel – often with only a handful of men, who created a deep but simple and lovely atmosphere of prayer. There were also more elaborate occasions, which made a deep impression on me, and ones which I think I'll never forget.

One such occasion was our week-long Wakefield Mission – my first and only experience of a mission "inside" and one which was very different indeed from any I had ever experienced, coming as I did from a traditional Catholic background. We had a team of six: Peter, the principal RC Chaplain in the prison service at that time; Maurice from the Bourne Trust in London; Gus, a former country and western singer; Dave, a recovered drug addict; John, a former nightclub bouncer; and Pete, a plumber and magician – a rare but powerful mixture indeed.

The team were out and about throughout the prison each day so the men had plenty of opportunity to talk to them. It amazed me and lifted my spirits greatly to see how many men were touched by the experience – men who, for the most part, had hitherto shown very little interest in the working of God in their lives. It was wonderful to see them open up and take steps – sometimes very falteringly – towards letting Jesus become a part of their lives. One man, Rob, said to me, "I know now that I have a friend who is always at my side and will never let me down. I have no need to fear ever again."

One of the team, Dave, came with me to Pinderfields Hospital in Wakefield one day to see two patients; one a prisoner and the other a prison officer. We must have looked a strange pair walking along the corridor – me in traditional garb and Dave with scraggy beard and ponytail and leather jacket – but we got a great welcome everywhere.

For me the highlight of each day was the evening gathering in the chapel, where the numbers increased as the week went on. We had lots of beautiful music and Bible songs (it was a delight to listen to Gus on the guitar) and the simple and moving stories heard at these gatherings brought a tear to many an eye. I think the abiding memory for me is the expression on the faces of the prisoners during these gatherings. There were men whom the media would call by all sorts of dreadful names. Yet, these were men who were finding the peace and the hope and the joy of knowing Jesus. These were men who were discovering the meaning of repentance and forgiveness. God certainly works in mysterious ways.

Needless to say, prayer was a very prominent feature of the week. Some prisoners invited members of the team to pray with them in their cells. It was a great support for us to know that many people throughout the country were praying for us including two Poor Clare communities, one in York and one in North Wales. A few nights before the Mission began we had a lovely Taizé Evening of prayer and praise. Many of the men would have loved to get together and pray each night but if they'd attempted to do that, the officers might well have concluded that they were up to no good and would certainly not have welcomed such an unusual assembly on the wings. For this reason one man, Mike, wrote what he simply called "The 10 o'clock prayer" and this was widely circulated among the men during the Mission. By the end of the week Wakefield Prison had become a powerhouse of prayer at 10.00pm. And to this day there are many men there who still recite the prayer at 10 o'clock. On occasions when I've been speaking to groups of people about prison ministry I've told them about this very special prayer and I've been glad to give them copies. I know that there are people in this country and even abroad who regularly pray this prayer. This is it.

Dear Lord, we pray that as this day draws to a close that you, Lord, draw us closer together in prayer and help us to face the many problems that challenge each one of us. Give us the wisdom to know that we do not face them alone for you are with us. And may your peace that goes beyond all human understanding strengthen and encourage, support and sustain us. And may we as brothers and sisters in Christ

Jesus share in each other's difficult times as well as the times of joy. And as we come to rest this night unite us all in the peace that only you are able to bring. We ask this in the name of your Son, our Lord and Saviour Jesus Christ, and the power of the Holy Spirit. Amen.

Originally Mike had written "And may we as brothers in Christ Jesus..." but I twisted his arm and got him to include the word "sisters". I find that sometimes when I'm standing at the bus stop on a morning this is a beautiful prayer to say, just changing the words a little so that it starts with "Dear Lord, we pray that as this day begins..."

Ash Wednesday marks the beginning of Lent and I recall a particular service we had on one occasion – ecumenical, as usual. I had asked one of the men, Steve, to give the homily and it was one I'll never forget. This was the gist of it: In prison we're all subject to searching. No one likes it but we have to accept it. However, there's a part of us that no one, no matter what his position in the prison, has authority to search and that is – the mind and heart of each of us. Only we can do that for ourselves. So, painful though the experience may be, Ash Wednesday provides us with an ideal opportunity of doing that.

Our Maundy Thursday ecumenical service has always been very special to me. We all begin together in the chapel with the Liturgy of the Word – the appropriate readings for the day, the homily, the inter-cessions, the Sign of Peace. Then we have the washing of the feet, a very symbolic gesture reminding us that Jesus washed the feet of his disciples on that first Holy Thursday night. Here I have to confess that I have rarely been able to get through this ceremony giving it the great degree of solemnity it is due. The reason is that when I come to wash the feet I usually get an uncontrollable urge to laugh – looking at the different shapes and sizes of the toes. I can't help noticing who it is who has washed his feet well and who it is who has been more than a little tardy in this respect. I can feel too that I'm not the only one with a smile on my face. Maybe the Lord has a smile on his face too. After this we separate and that's a painful thing, realising we cannot share the Eucharist together. It is one of those occasions which provide us with a great incentive to work for, and to pray more than ever for, Church unity. At this point I hold a Communion Service with the Catholic men in the congregation. Our number is small. We are gathered around a little table and I feel so aware of the atmosphere of the Last Supper. We reflect on Gethsemane and how Jesus must have felt before, during and after his arrest. Who better than the men in Wakefield to understand the feelings of a man in such a position and to empathise with him? I really feel that Christ is in our midst and looking after all of us no matter what may be in store. I find it an occasion of great hope.

Next comes Good Friday, but because of the prison regime we have our service at around 9.00am rather than the customary 3.00pm. Again, it's an ecumenical service and the highlight of that for me is the Veneration of the Cross which comes at the end. We invite any of the men who wish to do so, to come forward and kiss the cross. I explain that this is not idolatry but a symbolic action telling Jesus that we are sorry for all the ways in which we have offended him and that we will try to live our lives for him in the future. The hymn usually sung during this time is

"The Old Rugged Cross". I find it a most moving experience to see the men, many with tears in their eyes, come forward to kiss the cross. I've often found it hard to hold back the tears myself. How dear these men must be to God! We read in Scripture that God has no favourites but I wonder about that.

We try to mark Prisoners' Week with a service if possible. This is a week in late November set aside by the churches when we think of and pray for prisoners, ex-prisoners, their victims, their families and all those who work and minister in prison. I particularly remember a service some years ago – a service led by one of the men, to which we had invited a number of visitors from outside. The men themselves arranged the service and compiled the prayers. One prisoner wrote some music specially for the occasion. He told me he had stayed up practising until 1.30am the previous night. That can hardly have been conducive for good Christian relations as far as his neighbours were concerned. Our altar cloth had been embroidered by another prisoner. However, it had not started life as an altar cloth but as a bedspread. Unfortunately for Fred he had been required to relinquish it and so he happily presented it to us. During the service I saw him casting many an admiring glance at our newly acquired altar cloth.

A service of a different kind that stands out in my mind is saying the rosary during the month of May in honour of Our Lady. Men who come along on these occasions are mostly Catholics who have a tradition of great love and respect for Our Lady. I can clearly visualise the sun shining through the window on to our little altar. On it is a blue and white cloth embroidered by my mother and on that is a Nigerian statue of Our Lady given to me by my brother, Donal, who is a missionary in Nigeria. On the altar too is a candle brought to us from Lourdes by Joyce, a parishioner at the local Catholic church, St Austin's. This candle was by way of letting us know that she and her fellow pilgrims had prayed for all of us in Wakefield Prison when they had gone on pilgrimage to Lourdes with their kindly parish priest, Canon Barr. To make our altar complete we had a vase of lovely flowers. Here I must confess that I had "pinched" these from some flower beds around the prison and it was no small embarrassment to me to know that my actions in this respect had been recorded on camera. I'm sure I'm not allowed to say that the end justifies the means.

Not all the men who come along for a rosary gathering recite the rosary in the traditional way. Some use the rosary beads in a highly individual way (apart from the more common practice of wearing them round their necks). Ernie told me he uses his rosary beads regularly to count off the people he wants to pray for. He allocates one bead to each person and while he's fingering that particular bead he is praying for a particular person. I'm sure that good old St Dominic when he introduced us to the rosary hundreds of years ago never dreamed of the wonderful ingenuity of people like Ernie.

Some prisoners enjoy Bible Study, and particularly popular has been the Emmaus Bible Study correspondence course. I have been delighted to see men beaming with pride as they tell me they have got 85 percent or more on a paper. It's a huge incentive to them and provides a much-needed boost to morale.

The Alpha course, for anyone interested in finding out more about the Christian faith, is also popular as it gives those of us who do it an opportunity to get to know each other too. For me this close and regular contact is very enriching. I was really convinced of its value when one participant said that it had helped him to understand God and his forgiveness better, to understand himself better and to look more deeply into the causes of his offending behaviour with a view to doing something about it. I feel Alpha has done a lot of good for a lot of people in a lot of different ways.

Increasingly, because our chapel is a large, spacious and pleasant place it is being used for events which are not strictly religious but provide a positive experience for the men. One such occasion was a workshop entitled "Recognising the Positive". It was a unique gathering of prisoners, outside visitors, chaplains, a probation officer, members of the Board of Visitors and even some prison officers.

The beauty of it for me was that on this occasion we were all treated equally (and I think we all felt equal). The men did not have to return to their cells or the wings at lunchtime. Achieving this change from normal regime was not exactly the easiest thing in the world. All of us had lunch together in the chaplaincy and a delicious one it was too. I was well bribed not to tell the names of those who went up for second helpings. Mind you, it was a visitor, not a prisoner, who was first in the queue for the doughnuts.

In the morning, led by Pauline and Angus from "Scene Through Project", we had several ice-breaker exercises and gradually we were led into more demanding roles which made us reflect on our values and attitudes. This was done in a really interesting and amusing way and there was constant laughter in the air. What particularly delighted me was that on the occasions when I paused and quickly observed the people in the chapel, I noticed that all were smiling and seemed to be enjoying themselves thoroughly – even if sometimes we were making fools of ourselves at the same time. One example of that was when we sang "Old McDonald had a farm" in a multitude of forms and tones and voices.

When it came to the end of the afternoon we were exhausted with all the demands that had been made of us, but it was, I felt, a satisfied and worthwhile exhaustion. Maybe we learned a bit about ourselves and also about the difficulties people face regarding the dilemmas – moral and otherwise – of everyday life. I was impressed by the sharing, the openness and the honesty and I was so happy that the chapel and the chaplains were part of it.

11

Other Faiths

It's fascinating to be part of any religious team. It is even more fascinating to be part of a multi-faith group ministering in prison.

When a man enters prison he is asked for his religious denomination. For many men this is a straightforward question and they have little difficulty in giving the appropriate answer. Sometimes their answer is misheard and so they are given an incorrect registration. This can be later rectified. However, when a man comes into prison he may be feeling very frightened, hurt, angry or disturbed. His answer may be a contradiction of his religious denomination or belief. If he gives no answer, then, depending on the particular reception officer and the amount of time available, he may be registered as C of E or of nil religion.

I have learnt a lot from my inter-faith and multi-faith encounters in the prison. On one occasion I was informed that the Pagan minister was visiting. As I was the only chaplain on duty that day I felt I would be expected to meet him. This surfaced all sorts of negative feelings in me. What on earth would a pagan look like and what on earth would he have to say? I began to think of all sorts of good reasons why I was just too busy to meet him. Then I thought of my sister Kaye and her philosophy that everyone should be listened to rather than prejudged. I had the kettle boiling when Peter arrived and somewhat to my surprise I found him to be a charming man with a lot of good sense too. We had a cup of coffee and a great chat which was very enlightening.

One of my most memorable occasions was a lunch-time inter-faith meeting which we held in our multi-faith room. Present were the Christian chaplains and also the Muslim, Sikh and Jewish ministers. Preparing the food took some thought (we certainly didn't have any ham sandwiches). I remember too that our Mormon pastor had orange juice rather than tea or coffee. It was a most stimulating and enlightening exchange of ideas and the highlight for me was the few moments we spent together at the end in silent prayer and reflection. I knew all of us were praying for the men in Wakefield and God felt so close. What a wonderful experience of faith and hope and love.

I am always delighted to see any visiting minister of any denomination in the prison as I feel that person lifts the spirits of the men being visited. One afternoon I spotted an Orthodox Rabbi. I immediately approached him and with my hand extended to shake his hand I said, "You are most welcome, Rabbi, I am delighted to see you." He said "Thank you" but my hand remained suspended in the air and I was amazed to find he didn't shake hands with me. Later I was informed that this was because I was a woman. A year or two later, a prisoner asked to see a Rabbi. This was arranged and I went to meet him at the gate. Mindful of my former experience I greeted him but hesitated before extending my hand. When he took up his briefcase I got the message that handshakes were not in order so we chatted as I took him to the prisoner in the Healthcare Centre. There I introduced him to the prisoners and staff who were around at that time and he shook hands with each of them. Need I say, they were all male! He spent plenty of time there and had a good visit and later I took him to see another Jewish prisoner. As we walked along I said, "Rabbi, I have something to ask you. When I met you at the gate my natural inclination was to shake hands with you as part of our welcome. However, I felt such a gesture would not have been welcomed. Was I correct in my assessment of that situation?" He said that I was correct, and when I asked why this was so his reply was, "We have very high standards in our code of modesty and morality and to have shaken hands with you would have been the first step on the slippery slope." Well, that put me in my place but it also led me to read more and ask more questions about the Jewish faith so as to have an understanding of this somewhat unusual idea.

There was one occasion when we, the chaplaincy team, were visiting another prison. On our return to the car park our Muslim minister expressed his need to say his prayers. He asked if we could tell him where the south-east was. As the sun was shining at the time, I proudly told him I could work it out and shortly afterwards pointed him in a particular direction. He happily went off with his prayer mat and I happily boasted to my colleagues of my ability to work out where the south-east was. Almost immediately I realised my mistake. I had forgotten it was the afternoon and had calculated the direction assuming it was morning time. I hope God has forgiven poor old Mahomet and me too. By the way,

74

I never confessed my error to him when he returned.

Our Sikh ministers have always been friendly people. On the day before I began my prolonged leave of absence to look after my sick and elderly father in Ireland, I was chatting with the Sikh minister and telling him something of my great peace of mind. This was despite my apprehension about my ability to care for my father, knowing that I wasn't a cook, housekeeper or a nurse. I felt that my most difficult task would be trying to shave him. To this our Sikh remarked, "Why don't you ask him to become a Sikh and then he wouldn't have to be shaved at all!" The very suggestion of my poor old father becoming a Sikh brought a broad grin to my face and kept me smiling for the rest of the day. Incidentally I never did master the skill of shaving my poor old dad and I never could work out why he always started to yawn as soon as I got the razor near his mouth. There must be a message for me in it somewhere.

The richness of being in a multi-faith community! One man, Ben, was a keen – some would say over-keen – Catholic. I often felt he would have liked to see all prisoners and staff becoming Catholics. One day he asked if I would see a Jew who was in need of counselling. I had a good chat with this man and suggested I contact a Rabbi, to which he agreed. When my friend Ben heard about this he came along to me and said indignantly, "Glory be to God, Sister, you did the wrong thing. If you'd played your cards right, you could have made a Catholic out of him." When I tried to explain that would not be my intention he became even more indignant and threatened to write a letter of complaint to my bishop.

Then there was Jon who occasionally changed his religion. On one particular Jewish fast day he was, he said, practising the Jewish faith. The previous day he had established from me that Catholics are allowed only one meal on a fast day. When lunchtime came and Jon got the smell of hot food his ardour began to diminish a little – he asked the officer if there was food for him. The officer confirmed that there was food for him but whether or not he took it or kept his fast was his own decision. After a moment's hesitation Jon said, "I'll take the multi-faith approach and do it the Catholic way and have my dinner." I'd never blame Jon for such an action. I think I might have done the same myself!

I must tell you about Billy. Although he was not a churchgoer, Billy was very much an Irish Catholic at heart. At this particular time, curry was generally served only as part of the Muslim diet. One day Billy said to me, "Sister I want to become a Muslim. I think it's a lovely religion." I was quite surprised to hear this, given Billy's background, and asked him to tell me in what ways he considered it a lovely religion. To this he replied, "Ah Sister, don't be asking me awkward questions." I said, "Billy I'll only ask you one question. Is it because you like curry that you want to become a Muslim?" To this he replied, "Yes, but I'll always keep saying Hail Marys and stuff like that. And another thing Sister, you can call me Mahomet now, and not Billy." That gave me something to smile about for the rest of the day. When I saw him a few days later and greeted him with "Hello Mahomet" he replied sadly, "You can call me Billy again, Sister, as the Muslim man wouldn't have me." Poor old Billy. I'm delighted to say that soon afterwards curry became a part of the normal diet which greatly helped to minimise any "crisis of conscience" that folk like Billy might have.

12

A Free Day

Today was one of my free days. I like to come into the prison occasionally when I have no specific duty and can "loiter with intent" to my heart's content. It poured with rain all day and the wind was very high so it was no easy job locking and unlocking gates. Also, I gave up trying to use an umbrella (it has always struck me as odd that we are allowed to bring umbrellas into the prison but not something like a metal spoon). Going through the gate I saw a notice regarding a bed-watch in Pinderfields Hospital and I was glad to conclude from it that our prisoner dying of cancer was still alive.

My first stop was the Prison Officers' Association (POA) office for a little chat with the committee members there. They were preparing for a meeting about pay. They made me a nice cup of coffee and brought me up to date with some of the members who are on long-term sick leave. We put the world to rights in our own way. Next, I went to see an officer who had just returned to work after a long absence which was stress-related due to a traumatic incident in the prison. The macho image had slipped a bit, which was no harm, though I dare say it will soon reappear. Life is difficult at times but some of this difficulty can be of our own making.

There was just one letter for me – and a nice one it was too. Steve, who used to be in Wakefield and is now in another prison, wrote to say he'd got his BA and would be funded for an MA. I was delighted and immediately scribbled off a card to tell him so. I remembered the many dark days he had gone through in Wakefield and what great credit was due to him to have persevered with his studies.

I again braved the elements and visited a workshop. I enjoy visiting the many workshops because often men who will not engage in conversation on the wings will speak much more freely there. Sometimes, at the end of a shift, they ask me to help with their crosswords and I get a great kick out of being able to supply the missing word. However, today I wasn't able to do that but I don't think they held it against me. One man there, Sean, said he'd like a little chat so we chatted sitting on the bench beside his sewing machine. He told me he'd just heard that his brother-in-law had died in an accident. When I asked how it happened he said that his brother-in-law had been up to no good. He asked if he could come to chapel next week at the time of the funeral. He added, "To tell you the truth I don't say prayers and to tell you the truth I don't think I believe in God, but to tell you the truth I'd still love to come to the chapel next week." We're all different – no doubt about it.

It was great to have a free dinner hour. I listened to some nice music on Classic FM and phoned relatives of prisoners whom I normally wouldn't have time to ring. I was also able to study the list of applicants for our next Alpha course and this interested and pleased me too.

In the afternoon I took a jigsaw to Sam and had to make sure no pieces were missing. I also visited a number of Irishmen in preparation for a visit which hopefully we will soon have from the London-based priest who is the representative of the Irish Commission for Prisoners Overseas. This is a group set up by the Irish Hierarchy to help any Irish Nationals who may be in trouble overseas. Following this I had a long chat with a man whose case was very high profile, a man in whom I have seen an immense amount of good and yet one whose character and reputation are in shatters because of press vilification. How I wish I had more time to spend with people like this and how I wish I could communicate the real, genuine good I so often find.

My final visit was to the kitchen. If a prisoner has money we can arrange for him to send out flowers for a special occasion to his family or a girlfriend. Mark who worked in the kitchen wanted to send flowers to his wife for her birthday. When I arrived I said to the officer in charge, "Is it okay if I sort out a flower order with Mark?" Normally he would have said "That's fine", but today he looked at me strangely. The look surprised me until I realised he thought I was speaking of a "flour" order and was wondering what on earth we were doing with flour in the chaplaincy!

I went home tired and drenched to the skin, but happy.

13

More Random Thoughts

Some people without ever knowing it make a great contribution to the wellbeing of prisoners. One such person is a neighbouring parishioner called Auntie Sheila (I got to know her through her niece Ann). Auntie Sheila regularly supplies me with bundles of a magazine called *Irelands Own,* a collection of short stories, riddles, songs, jokes and articles of a general nature. These I am allowed to distribute in the Block and they are a rare treat for the men there. I sometimes think that my value is measured by whether or not I have a supply of *Irelands Own* in my green, white and orange Lifestyle plastic bag. On one occasion a man said, "Have you seen Mrs Durkan lately?" I was somewhat taken aback until I realised he'd spotted Auntie Sheila's name on the front of a magazine and as he hadn't had a copy of *Irelands Own* for some time he was gently hinting that I might remind her of his need. I know that Auntie Sheila prays for these men too and, as I so often say, folk like her are the salt of the earth.

Then there's Sr Colette, who visits the prison on occasions. One of the men, Richard, discovered that they both come from Cork and great was his joy when she sent him a card from there. Her ministry involves a lot of travel so Richard gets many a card which he proudly shows me, invariably saying each time "How nice of her to think about me!" Indeed one of the many positive things that strikes me about prison visitors is the way in which, when on holiday, they remember their prisoner friends and send postcards which are so often worth their weight in gold. On one occasion when a prison visitor sent a birthday card to Wayne he told me he now had four cards. I said that was great as obviously three other people thought about him too. His reply was, "No, that's not it. The other three were the ones my Mam sent for the last three years before she died, and that was ten years ago." On another occasion I was chatting with a young man called Ray. He told me it was his birthday. I asked if he'd got any card at all and he said he hadn't had a card or a birthday celebration since he was 10 years old. Needless to say, I made sure he was in possession of a birthday card before the day was out.

Hairstyles always fascinate me. The barber comes into Wakefield regularly so the men have plenty of opportunity to see him and they don't have to pay him either! When I see a man with a nice haircut I like to comment on it, being well aware that I may be the only female who makes such a comment to him. On more than one occasion I have seen men blush when I've told them how well their new hairstyle suits them. Sometimes hairstyles sadden me. I see them as attempts by some men to help them cope with what they find as a very difficult situation. I have seen this especially in the cases of men who have held high professional positions before coming into prison. I think of two men in particular who had very striking heads of hair and who chose to have haircuts which left them almost bald. I think of another man who grew his hair in a pigtail which was very much contrary to his usual hairstyle. In each case I think it helped the prisoner to blend in more easily with his new background.

Some time ago I had a strange request. A Rastafarian who had just cut off his dreadlocks told me he had done so as a mark of respect for his two babies who had died cot deaths four and six years previously. His dreadlocks were in a plastic bag in his cell. He wanted me to arrange to have them buried in the grave where his children were buried. It no longer amazes me to hear what people need to bring them peace of mind.

Thinking of peace of mind reminds me too of how amazed I first felt – and still do – to see how prisoners can sometimes continue to smile even in the midst of the greatest difficulties. They seem to have a resilience which I find truly surprising, a sort of philosophical outlook on life which would seem to say, "Society has done its worst but I won't let it get me down." Not all prisoners are of this disposition and the scene behind the closed door of a man's cell may tell a different story, but I truly marvel at the positive way so many men deal with their very, very difficult situations.

People have asked me how I fit in, in such an alien milieu. "What a contrast to convent life," they say. However, I really feel very much at home in Wakefield. Prison regimes were for a long time based on a monastic rule of life, and so many aspects of prison life, such as censorship, constantly asking permissions, and big "spring cleaning" before Christmas and Easter were all once very much part of our lifestyle too. Nowadays there might be within the prison walls about

1000 people: staff, prisoners, visitors. I always feel perfectly free to greet each one of them and in almost every case receive a cheery greeting and smile in return. I consider that a great blessing and I just wonder where else in the world such a response could be expected by just an ordinary person like me.

14
Christmas

Most people of my acquaintance appear to look forward to Christmas, the time of peace and goodwill they say. However, the more you talk to people the more their Christmas-related problems seem to surface. These problems have to do with money, who's going to visit who for Christmas dinner, toys for the children, lack of time for preparing, even with extra opening times at the stores, lack of energy and so on, not to mention parties which are meant to be enjoyable experiences. These problems may not always be major ones but they are enough to create tensions which often lead to arguments and rows. Such is the nature of our human condition. This is an area in life that the men in prison do not always appreciate. Their vision of Christmas on the "outside" seems to be one of sweetness and light, which doesn't measure up to reality but which makes their position seem even more lonely to themselves and makes Christmas on the whole a bad time.

A short time before Christmas, I met a lady who would generally be considered a pillar of the Church in our diocese. I know her to be kind, generous and hardworking in her services to the Church. She enquired what Christmas would be like in prison and I explained to her something of the loneliness which the men would experience. She replied, "You know my views. I'd have them all hung up or else locked up and the key thrown away." That comment made me feel very sad indeed, coming as it did from her. I suppose we all have our blind patches. On another occasion, again shortly before Christmas, I visited a good friend of mine. She asked if I knew a particular prisoner whose case had been very high profile in the media. I mentioned a couple of very good things which I knew about this man but she would have none of it and was absolutely scathing in her wholesale condemnation of him, merely using the information she'd picked up from the media. This too saddened me very much. How I would love to be able to "educate" such people.

A third negative experience I had was on my way back to the prison on Christmas Eve, having visited a prisoner, Alan, who was dying. The radio was on in the car and there were carols being sung. By way of conversation with the driver (my thoughts were really still with Alan) I said, "Do you like carols?" His reply was, "I don't, and to be truthful I don't think anyone really does." That reply really surprised me and made me reflect sadly on how negative his experiences of carol singing and the real beauty of the Christmas story must have been.

However, Christmas Eve did have a wonderful experience for me, one which energised me for the whole of my day in prison. As is my usual practice when I go to prison, I headed for St Austin's Church in Wakefield for the 7.45am Mass. I was disappointed as I approached to notice that the place was in

85

darkness. However, what a surprise awaited me as I opened the door. The church was indeed in darkness but there in a pool of light on the altar was the monstrance containing the Blessed Sacrament. It was surrounded by a circle of nightlights and underneath the altar was the beautiful crib. It was breathtaking and I was so grateful that I'd caught the early bus from Leeds that morning, which meant I had fifteen minutes of adoration before Mass. It was a time too when I remembered my family, my Community, and needless to say, all those in prison, especially three or four of the men who had particular needs at that time. We had Mass by candlelight and by the time it was over at 8.15, the natural morning light had gently come through – a reminder of how gently God comes into our world. The priest, Fr Nunan, reminded us, the congregation, to carry God's light to all we met that day; he also reminded us that God is credible in the world if he is credible in us. It was a message I tried to take to heart on that Christmas Eve in my encounter with so many wounded people.

Now let me tell you something of what Christmas in the prison itself was like. Many of the staff and prisoners try to show something of the Christmas spirit, but it is a very difficult environment in which to do this. Christmas is a strange time – a time of contradiction – in prison and I think this Christmas was typical of most. It's a time when we think particularly of family – a thought which often brings to the surface a lot of sadness, guilt, loneliness and disappointment in prisoners. On the other hand, it is a time when the afternoon visiting times are filled to capacity, when the Christmas cards pour in and when giant Christmas cards, coming in and going out, can be seen in profusion. This Christmas was no exception and the centre and the wings were full of traditional decorations including Christmas trees. The men's attitudes varied, some really pleased that an attempt had been made to introduce the Christmas spirit, and others really sad because they felt it emphasised for them still further the gap that existed between them and their families.

The subject of food was frequently discussed and many of the men really welcomed the extra quality, quantity and variety which Christmas brought. One man, Alan, in the Segregation Unit, told me on Boxing Day that he had gone to bed contented for the first day since arriving in prison because he had enjoyed his food so much. Another man also in the Block told me that there were actually eleven items on the menu that day which he particularly enjoyed. I was really pleased to hear this, being conscious of how much I also enjoy my food. Needless to say, there were also a few grumbles and I was amazed to hear one man complain because he had only got grapefruit and bacon and sausage for his breakfast. I felt he did much better than I did with my toast and coffee, but then I ate my breakfast against a background of freedom and that made all the difference in the world.

A few days before Christmas we had a lovely carol service – ecumenical as usual. It was my turn to give the homily and I was so pleased to be able to remind the men that Jesus came on earth knowing what he was taking on in saving us, yet knowing that each of us was worth it. Coming on earth for us meant that even as a baby he was on the run in the flight into Egypt, trying to escape from Herod. He was often treated with indifference and injustice. He was spied on, betrayed, denounced and arrested by the High Priests. He was locked up in Jerusalem.

He was put on trial. I think many of the prisoners could identify with some of this and I prayed that it would give them hope. We had many visitors who joined prisoners, staff and chaplains, and we all had a great chat afterwards over a cuppa and a mince pie. Need I say that the singing of the carols was out of this world. The men seem to put their whole heart and soul into the singing and I'm sure that through it there is a lot of healing. I think that the praise that ascends to God from that chapel must be sweet music in his ears and must move him to look with special kindness on these men. One visitor told me that she had heard Huddersfield Choral Society sing "Messiah", the Bach Choir sing in London, and many other famous choirs, but none had inspired her so much as the singing of the men in Wakefield Prison.

There were two people who surprised me by their absence. I knew them to be men of faith and men of prayer and I felt somewhat anxious about them. Later I went to have a little chat with each. One told me he'd been present at the Hillsborough disaster and ever since has been unable to cope with crowds. The other told me that he finds carol services highly emotional occasions and he felt he would be unable to get through the service without weeping, which he didn't feel was a situation he could handle easily. Isn't it strange that we sometimes easily forget that these men are subject to the same kinds of reactions as the rest of us mortals? I said a special prayer that night for both of those men.

Christmas is generally a time for celebrating and for quite a number of people that means consuming a fair amount of alcohol. Naturally alcohol is forbidden in prison but this does not deter some of the more determined men from trying to produce it. One man whom I met in the Segregation Unit a few days before Christmas was there because he had been discovered making hooch. With a twinkle in his eye he said, "Well, they caught me this time Sister, but there will be other times!" What can you say to that?

One man, John, had a big grin on his face as I went to his door in the Block. He invited me to admire his Christmas decorations. He had about six cards on his wall – stuck on with toothpaste (how else could he stick them on?). He had a white twisted garland, made from toilet paper, going round his cell, and little white blobs of snow, also made from toilet paper, stuck – again with toothpaste – on his windows. I really had to admire his spirit and it led me to marvel at how resilient the human spirit can be. Christmas is an amazing time, no doubt about it, and the spirit of hope that lives in John will be an inspiration to me for a long time.

15

A Happy Conclusion

Today was a long day. I entered the prison at 8.30am and left at 7.30pm. I arrived a little earlier to attend a staff meeting but this was cancelled because of a POA pay-related meeting, following which the officers arrived late at the gate causing a great delay. Even the outside contractors working in the prison had to remain outside until the officers had gone through. I always think what a dreadful waste of time and money that is. But then, is there any other way to sort thorny problems out? I don't know.

Because of this delay, the prisoners were not in circulation until about an hour later than usual. I used this time to have a cuppa and a nice little chat with the other chaplains, Alan and Terry, and then did some individual letters of welcome for the members of our new Alpha course. I also helped to put away the crib – an over-due job – and wondered where I'll be at Christmas next year.

Later I went to the Healthcare Centre where I was given another cuppa, and found the men generally to be in good form, which unfortunately is not a regular experience. There was plenty of conversation and I spoke at length with a man who was full of apprehension at the prospect of being released soon. He was particularly terrified at the thought of dealing with traffic. One man called across the room, "Will you ask Fr Malachy to come and hear my confession? I haven't been for ages." A man nearby shouted, "And you need it badly too!" which resulted in big smiles all around.

One new patient in the Healthcare Centre bore a striking resemblance to a former prisoner, and as I left, my thoughts went back to that former prisoner. He had held a very high ranking office in his particular religion which was pretty fundamentalist, and because a girl in his congregation had misbehaved he took an active part in causing her death. I could never see any remorse whatsoever in that man. He believed he was doing God's will. I know it's being judgmental to say so, but I believe it is men like that who are really dangerous. Another group of really dangerous men, in my opinion, are the child molesters who say they love children. They, for the most part, really believe this too and so often they will not, or cannot, accept responsibility for their offences. They certainly need our prayers. I was still reflecting on all of this when I arrived on the wings.

After a short visit to the wings in unsuccessful pursuit of an officer called Sam, whose wife I knew to be very ill, I returned to the chaplaincy for our monthly team meeting which lasted from midday until 2.00pm. Our team consists of Alan, Terry, Malachy, Peter, Gordon, Meredith and myself, and there's always plenty to talk about. Today we were joined for a short while by George, the Principal Officer in Security. He brought us up to date with issues in his department and very interesting they were too. One of my little jobs is to write up the minutes of these meetings. The chair of the meeting revolves annually between Catholic, Anglican and Methodist chaplains and that brings an interesting and different dimension.

Following the meeting two of us went out to visit Wakefield Hospice. Sometimes it's nearly as hard getting out of the prison as getting in, but we managed it! As we were going into the hospice, who did we meet but Sam, the officer whom I'd failed to track down in the prison earlier on. His wife is now in the hospice too and of course we visited her. It made me reflect on what a heavy burden Sam must have been carrying for many a day while still doing a demanding job very professionally. We then went to see Jamie, which was the main purpose of our visit. Jamie is a prison officer, very ill indeed but someone who is full of life. He has a unique personality and is highly respected not only by his colleagues but by prisoners too. He is not what you would call, or he would call, a religious person in the usual meaning of the word. However, when I reminded him that one of the prisoners, Eddie, had told me that he says a prayer for him each night, Jamie's eyes filled with tears. I was again reminded of how much we can all help each other no matter who we are, what we are or where we are. We might be wounded healers but we are still healers. We spoke too with Jamie's family who were there and assured them of our prayers.

Following this visit we walked across to Pinder-fields Hospital. (Pinderfields Hospital is a very difficult place to park. An officer and I once visited a sick member of staff there and when we came out we had a £20 fine clapped on the windscreen.) Here we visited Alan, a prisoner dying of cancer. He was extremely ill and I doubt I'll see him again. However, on each occasion for the past few months when I've seen him, I doubted he would survive 24 hours and yet he is still with us. There are still two officers on duty with him, which I personally consider quite unnecessary for many reasons although this view is not shared by the powers that be. Thank God the handcuffs have been removed at last. Some officers on duty are kind and compassionate, some are uncaring. I can't say that I felt on top of the world as I left the hospital.

We returned to the prison, again going through all the searching procedures. I delivered the Alpha letters prepared earlier and then got ready for my evening meeting. After a nice cuppa and a piece of fruit (well, two pieces if I'm to be honest) I put my feet up and said my Evening Prayer as I would not be able to join my Community at home at our regular time. Needless to say the needs of the prison were included in those prayers and especially the needs of the three very ill people we'd visited.

After a little chat with the PE instructor who was testing the alarms in the chaplaincy and also the gym which is above the chaplaincy, I went to my evening meeting which was on "Dealing with Bereavement", an interesting meeting indeed. The men spoke of their grief and their sadness, all very much compounded by their guilt. I know some of these men have committed some dreadful offences but I don't think many people realise the pain and the sorrow and the deep, deep sadness which enshrouds them – sometimes for ever.

However, all was not sadness today. I heard two pieces of good news. Barry, a prisoner from the south told me that his mother had bought herself some new shoes and at the same time entered a competition. She won, and as a result received holiday vouchers and spending money worth hundreds of pounds. I was really happy for her, as she's a lovely lady. I was very happy for Barry too. The other bit of good news came from Liz, our librarian, who told me that she had arranged for an Irish band, Black Velvet, to come into the prison. I knew the men would be thrilled and so was I. They have given us a concert on a previous occasion, a lively one it was too and thoroughly enjoyed by the men. There was much clapping and tapping of feet to the familiar and lively tunes and the young man beside me said, "All I'm missing now is a pint of Guinness in my hand." I was sorry I couldn't oblige.

I had only one letter today and that was from Terry, a former Wakefield man now in another prison, to tell me his mother had died. He also had the good news that he had become a grandfather, which I was thrilled to hear, knowing how eagerly he'd awaited that day. He said that being in prison had made him a "mite institutionalised" and that events since he last wrote were "like the Grand National with fences coming up so rapidly... up and down, up and down". He finished up by saying, "I am fully aware of the Power which has looked over me during the last ten years." That comment was good enough to bring the day to a happy conclusion for me.

16

The Grim Reaper

Death is a mystery but the mystery seems to be even deeper when the death relates to someone connected with prison. From men who have themselves caused death, often very violently, you might expect a view that sets less value on human life than the norm and perhaps a more "earthy" view of death. On the contrary, for a prisoner to receive news of the death of a close relative can be a most devastating blow even if the death was expected or even if they have not been in contact for many years. Added to the shock and the sadness can be a huge amount of guilt. One of the most difficult tasks I have as a chaplain is to inform a man of the death of his child or his parent or other close member of his family.

One occasion that will always remain with me was when I had to tell Michael of the death of his daughter who had died from drugs. She had a six-year-old daughter and a baby who had been born an addict. The situation was made worse by the fact that Michael was separated from his wife and so it was difficult to find out all the information surrounding her death. All he could repeat was, "This would never have happened if I was outside to look after her." I talked with Michael many times during the next few days when he showed me photos of his beloved "little girl" and recalled many fond memories. He was escorted to the funeral in handcuffs, as is the norm. When he met his family briefly afterwards his little granddaughter ran up to him to hug him, but when she saw the handcuffs she cried in fright and ran away from him. It's hard to imagine the depth of the sadness of that man as he arrived back to his cell in the prison.

A number of men have died in prison while I have been a chaplain there and such deaths are far from easy to cope with for most of us. On one occasion a man was murdered, someone I'd spoken to earlier that same day. The following day I had to see the man responsible who by that time was in the Seg-regation Unit. That was a meeting I found very difficult indeed. It was a big learning experience for me too in terms of empathising with victims. On another occasion I spoke with a man who had almost succeeded in murdering a member of staff. I actually challenged him (though my legs were quaking) and said I couldn't understand how one human being could treat another like that. He smiled, but it was a smile that never reached his eyes, and replied, "You wouldn't understand, Sister Carmel." I don't know if that encounter did him any good at all but it certainly got something off my chest and made me feel better.

In my first years in the prison, funerals of prisoners tended to be in Wakefield cemetery though in recent times they have taken place in the crematorium. The first funeral I attended was that of Lawrence, a man who often boasted of his many rich relatives. Sadly nobody claimed the body for burial or showed up at the funeral on that bright May morning as the birds were singing and the trees were a magnificent shade of green. I thanked God that Lawrence was buried there and prayed that he would have peace – a peace that he never seemed to be able to find in the prison.

Then I think of Harry, buried in that same cemetery. For "next of kin", Harry had given his son's name and address. However, Harry died very suddenly and it was soon found that the address he had given for his son was non-existent. It would appear that he didn't want it to be known that he had lost contact with his son and really didn't know his address at all.

About six months later I received a phone call from Harry's son, who was devastated. He had visited his father while on remand in Strangeways but couldn't handle it when he received a prison sentence. It was only by accident that he discovered his father had died. Between his tears he spoke of the beautiful plants he would put on his dad's grave, and said that he would always tend it carefully, but that could never make up for the guilty and empty feelings he experienced because of deserting his father in his hour of need. He too needs our prayers for healing.

It's beautiful to witness the support that prisoners can give to each other. David was a man who had but one relative in this country and he was a very high-ranking army officer who appeared to want nothing whatsoever to do with David. No doubt he too had his own story. However, I had hoped in vain that he would turn up at David's funeral as he had been informed of the time and place. There was nobody present other than the undertaker, our Anglican chaplain, and myself. On David's coffin was a simple arrangement of flowers with a card which read "From your friends who cannot be here today". I still have that card, hoping perhaps that a day will come when David's brother feels able to talk about him. I can let him know that although his brother was a prisoner he didn't die without friends.

The death of Les will always remain in my memory. He had been ill in our hospital with cancer for quite a long time. Although he had a family he had no wish whatsoever to contact them. On the whole, staff were good to him. One day Les said that what he would really love above anything else was an egg buttie. Such a luxury could not at that time be obtained from the kitchen. A kind officer, Ian, looked at me knowingly and said he would see to it. When I saw Les next day he had had his egg buttie and said that it was the nicest one he had ever tasted in his whole life. Ian had gone beyond the call of duty but it was a truly lovely human gesture.

Les had found great comfort in his faith in his latter days and had said many times that this would be his greatest comfort when dying. He was eventually taken to outside hospital and I was so happy to see him so very clean and tidy in a bed with lovely clean white sheets. One morning a few days later I went into the prison to find the whole place shut down so that detailed searches could be made. This was shortly after the Manchester Strangeways riot. Not particularly wanting to spend the whole morning on paperwork I rang the hospital and was told that Les was dying. On a sudden impulse I rang his prison visitor, Sr Stephanie, who by a strange chain of coincidences, was at home that morning. Very shortly afterwards we met up at Les's bedside. He was conscious but breathing with difficulty and he died peacefully as we sat beside him and held his hand. It was a blessed moment for Les, for Stephanie and for me. I'm sure Les heard in his heart the final prayer we said as we commended his soul to God.

Another death-bed scene which I shall never forget was when Peter, a prison officer, died. Peter had been ill with cancer for a very long time and had been nursed most lovingly at home by his wife Kitty. I always marvelled at the wonderful bond between them. On the night Peter died we had had our carol service in the prison. It had been a long day for me from the time I'd stood at the bus stop at 7.00am until the time I'd arrived home at 8.00pm, and I was more than ready for my dinner. Some time later I had a phone call from Kitty to say Peter was dying, and I had promised to be with them then if it was at all possible. I'd been a regular visitor to their home over several months and had enjoyed their company and hospitality on many occasions – they were a delightful couple.

When I arrived that night Peter was very ill but conscious. I told him that I had come from the Carol Service and that Jeremy, a prisoner whom Peter had helped a lot, had composed and sung a carol. A little smile crossed his lips and he said "Very nice." Even in his last illness Peter could still be pleased by the positive deeds of a prisoner. Knowing that Peter was near the end, I asked Kitty if she would like me to say the Lord's Prayer. She said yes and we prayed it together. At the end Peter whispered "Amen." Kitty then said, "Peter, I'd like a kiss," and I watched with tears in my eyes as he lifted his thin little head, pouted his lips and kissed her. Then he lay back on the pillow and peacefully died. It was a beautiful death and I felt so privileged to be present at that awesome moment. It was a privilege for me too to be invited to take his funeral service, though the procession at the beginning of the service must have seemed a somewhat unusual sight with a veil-clad Irish Catholic Sister walking in front of the Union Jack-draped coffin.

On the day following that particular funeral, to my surprise and delight, I was made an honorary member of the POA. I have worn the badge on two occasions, once when I was giving the homily at the funeral of a young prison officer who died very tragically, and the other when I went to Buckingham Palace to receive the Butler Award.

Death is a grim reaper. On one occasion an older man died of a heart attack in his cell. It was almost noon and the comment made by an officer on that wing was "Well, that's one less for dinner." Then there was a prisoner, Malcolm, who was taken out to his mother's funeral but because of some mix-up he arrived at the wrong funeral; his mother's funeral had taken place the previous day. Speaking to Malcolm later in the day, I could see a man who was struggling greatly with a huge amount of frustration and anger, and above all, sadness.

What has particularly saddened me were the consequences of some men dying in our local hospice. Now the hospice has been wonderful to these men and brought tremendous enrichment and peace into their last hours. However, when some of the local media got hold of the knowledge that these Wakefield prisoners were there, a lot of hatred and anger was whipped up in the local community which was deeply disturbing to prisoners and their families. My dream is that we would have a little hospice within the prison itself, where men could die with dignity. Surely it's not too much to hope for. I want to keep that dream alive, and I pray that one day it will become a reality.

"O death where is your victory?" That's a question I often ask myself when a prisoner dies in custody. It's a moving and sad – sometimes very sad – situation. I certainly wouldn't like it to happen to me or to anybody belonging to me. On the other hand, our God is a God not only of justice but of mercy. On many an occasion when prisoners tell me of their sorrow for what they have done and of some of their deepest thoughts and feelings I feel almost overwhelmed by a strong sense of how very dear and precious those men must be to God. He who died on the cross for love of each one of us knows that whatever the suffering they may have caused they have also themselves suffered, sometimes enormously and relentlessly, for year after year after year. What a comfort to know that God sees the heart. Death can be a release from prison, and not just in a physical way. It can be the beginning of a peace and a joy and a happiness that has seemed an impossible dream for most of a man's life. From being a 'Grim Reaper' death can be transformed into a Liberating Saviour.

17
Wakefield Extension

In the early part of this year National Express Coach Company made a fantastic offer to the "over 50s" – a return journey to anywhere in the country for £9.99. I decided to avail myself of it for my mini-busman's (or buswoman's) break. I certainly got value for money.

The first stage of my journey was Leeds to London Victoria where I had a couple of hours to spend before my connection to Worthing. Now, two hours provided me with the time and opportunity to meet the mother of a prisoner and to have a good chat over a lovely hot cuppa. Louise's ready smile and beautiful soft Scottish accent belied the great sadness she carried. She told me about Jamie's childhood, his strong academic achievements and his phone call in the middle of the night which heralded the terrible offence resulting in the death of a young man whom he had attacked. That was the beginning of a real hell for Louise, a kind, gentle and refined woman – the trial, the conviction and now the regular prison visits. Because of that midnight phone call to her many years ago, Louise now unplugs the phone every night even though she knows Jamie cannot phone her at that time. She's in a second marriage so understandably her husband does not have the same interest in Jamie as she has. She really values her visits to prison and any little bit of private time she has at home in which to think her own thoughts and to listen to music which brings her Jamie to mind. Occasionally she and her husband go away at weekends. If they get into conversation with fellow travellers and talk about family, she mentions her other son, Brian, but doesn't talk about Jamie despite the fact that he is in the forefront of her mind. She told me about a letter she received some time ago from the mother of Jamie's victim. The anguish of this poor woman caused her an enormous amount of anguish too. If suffering were a passport to Heaven, mothers like Louise would be at the head of the queue.

The coach journey from London to Worthing was pleasant and I had a lovely welcome from our Sisters there, who as usual were full of interest and full of questions about prison work. One of the community had just come home from her weekly stint helping at a hostel for the homeless and her highlight that night had been her encounter with an ex-prisoner. She said she hoped he wasn't an escapee from Ford, a prison I was visiting the following day. Needless to say, the Sisters in Worthing pray regularly for prisoners and for all who look after them and I always feel that their prayers are a great support.

Next day I went to HMP Ford and as ever had a lovely visit with Ian, who used to be in Wakefield. This was my first visit to an open prison, though I have visited quite a number of other prisons housing ex-Wakefield men when my duties as a Sister have taken me to convents in fairly close proximity. I was absolutely amazed at the degree of "openness" in an open prison and wondered if I would have enough willpower not to try to escape if I were a prisoner. Ian had been on a town visit a couple of weeks previously and I was interested to hear that the things that struck him most were the number of shops selling mobile phones and the number of shops selling sports gear. We had a good chat on a wide variety of topics including what I might or might not include in this book. I always find it interesting and enriching to view things from a prisoner's perspective. It helps me to keep my feet on the ground.

Next morning I had the bonus of a lovely walk by the sea – a rare experience which I always thoroughly enjoy. I then set off on my National Express coach from Worthing to Portsmouth. There I was met by a former Wakefield Methodist chaplain, David, and his wife Zoya, who took me to lunch. Wakefield Prison was never far from our thoughts and it did me good to chat with them. They then brought me to the home of Sr Annunciata (whom I have already mentioned) and Sr Anna, with whom I would be staying for two nights. These two Sisters, who have done more for prisoners in Portsmouth and their families than anyone else I know, are looking after homeless men and providing them with jobs on their little farm. Well, one hour before I arrived they had given my bed to a very sick man who had been discharged from hospital and who had nowhere else to go. As always I got a great welcome and a comfortable spot to sleep in, my only disturbance being a very noisy cock who for some strange reason began to crow in the middle of the night and never stopped until morning. Added to this, they had a cow which was expected to calve any time and Sr Anna insisted that if that were to happen in the middle of the night she would call me out to help her deliver the calf. I was very relieved indeed not to be a participant in such a novel experience.

My visit to Kingston Prison in Portsmouth was good as usual. I well remember the reason for my first visit to Kingston over 20 years ago. A prisoner called Paul had been moved there from Wakefield. Shortly afterwards I had a letter from a Sacred Heart Sister saying she'd met Paul who had told her I was very anxious to visit him (not true!) but I'd nowhere to stay. She wrote to offer me a bed for the night. Some time later I had business in the area and availed myself of the opportunity to see Paul. (I had to give him full marks for being cheeky!) I particularly enjoy visiting Kingston as there are so many old friends there from Wakefield. It feels like home from home as I encounter these men. I've almost forgotten some of their faces and I've certainly forgotten some of their names, but it's always so lovely to see them. We had a great chat and a nice cuppa in the education department. There was so much to say that the time just flew. One of the men, Harold, brought down some photographs. Now, I love photos and these were particularly interesting. There were graduation photos of himself and I felt so pleased for him and so proud of him as I studied them. Then there were photos of the most recent marathon where I recognised a number of old friends in the familiar grounds of Kingston. Lastly, Harold showed me some wedding photos of ex-Wakefield man Jim, now in another prison, who certainly cut a dash in his wedding suit. What a contrast from prison uniform. Harold had been best man, so the photos looked quite splendid. I don't think marriages in prison are a good idea at all, but I certainly hope and pray that Jim and his wife will be very happy.

Following this visit I went to that section of the prison where the elderly reside, hoping to meet Reg, who had left Wakefield a year or two before. I remembered him as a kind old gentleman who always courteously stood up when I arrived at the cell which he shared with his old friend Brian, and a younger man, Juiian, who was dying of cancer, as I've already mentioned. I was anxious to see how Reg was coping and I had promised to give Brian a detailed account of my visit on my return to Wakefield. It was with sadness that I was told that Reg had died about six months earlier. It wasn't easy to report back to Brian, nor to Bob, another old friend of Reg's. I was consoled, however, by their comments that at least he had had some time to enjoy the amenities of Kingston, and that he had now gone to a better place.

On the bus back to Sr Annunciata's and Sr Anna's home, I prayed that the calf would have been born before I returned, but alas my prayer wasn't answered! However, my next prayer was heard – namely that the calf wouldn't be born in the middle of the night. I could cope with the cock crowing but not with the cow calving. I think I could cope more easily with a night in a prison cell!

Next morning I attended a beautiful Mass at Park Place Pastoral Centre nearby. All the Sisters whom I met there were Indian, the celebrant had an Indian vestment and the whole liturgy had a decided Indian flavour. One of the lovely things there for me was that they did pray specially for prisoners. I am always heartened and encouraged when I think of the number of people who pray for prisoners.

My journey back to Leeds was a long one – I

certainly got value for my £9.99 ticket. Sitting for so many hours on the coach I was in very close proximity – in fact shoulder to shoulder – to others. What if any of them had been on drugs? My clothing could easily have been contaminated. I washed everything as soon as I got home but should I have gone as a visitor straight from my journey into Wakefield it's not impossible that the drug dog would have sat down in front of me indicating that he had detected drugs. It made me appreciate even more how very difficult it can be at times for family and friends travelling by public transport to see their loved ones in prison. In fairness though, it has to be said that our little drug dog has done an excellent job in helping us all work towards a more drug-free prison.

My journey was an enjoyable one. May God bless National Express and their £9.99 special offer. Long may it last.

18
Tomorrow is Another Day…

A lovely sunny morning despite the chill in the air. Once again the weather provides an easy topic of conversation as I enter the prison. This morning we have to be searched in the Visitors' Entrance, which means our shoes have to be taken off too – just one more of the myriad delays which punctuate our day. If you are not endowed with an abundance of patience, life can be very difficult in prison.

I make my way to the post room in the Admin Block where I post a card to Steve, a former Wakefield man now in another prison. This is to congratulate him and his companions on their excellent production for Sunday Worship on national TV yesterday. It is so heartening to see things like that. My next port of call after coffee with my colleagues is the kitchen to collect fruit juice and biscuits for our next Alpha session. A morning visit to the kitchen is always a special experience. I see what appear to be millions of potatoes, already cooked at 10.00am, stacks and stacks of loaves of bread, hundreds of buns for tea time, cauldrons of bubbling beans, and mounds of really lovely-looking fresh vegetables, especially the magnificent heads of cabbages. There's enough salad to feed about 600 people and in spite of the busyness of staff and prisoners in there, there is always a lot of banter. I'm offered plenty of jobs, especially in the washing-up department, but these I graciously decline. My kitchen qualifications, apart from sampling food, leave a lot to be desired.

Having deposited my goodies in the chaplaincy I head back to the wings, on my way encountering our Dispersals Director, a very important visitor to our establishment. I congratulate him on his new appointment as Assistant Director General of the Prison Service, and as I am always anxious to seize an opportunity when I get one I remind him of our last conversation when we discussed the possibility of having a hospice in Wakefield Prison. Hopefully, in due course, he'll see his way to making this dream come true. On the wings I meet David, a Jew, for whom I've promised to find out the date of Passover this year, Tony, for whom I've organised a Bourne Trust visitor, Steve, for whom I've got a jigsaw (it had to be 750 pieces with none missing), and Peter, to whom I've promised a book on Celtic spirituality. On my travels through the wings I meet a lady from the Parole Board. I am delighted with my good luck as there are several questions I wanted to ask her about parole, tariff dates, etc. I find her answers a bit evasive and am not much the wiser after our little chat.

I next go to the Healthcare Centre to see Paul. I had been particularly concerned about Paul the previous day as I understood he had taken an overdose, having paid a half ounce of tobacco to another prisoner, Andy, in exchange for Andy's tablets. To my amazement I find that Paul has just arrived back from the Block having been before the Governor and been given a fine for procuring someone else's tablets. Now, whilst I in no way want to minimise the nature of Paul's offence in procuring Andy's tablets, I feel strongly that his need for help was greater than the need to be punished. I bring this matter to a Governor and am told that Paul had got those tablets not to harm himself but to "get a buzz"! Where the truth of the matter is, I don't know.

After my coffee and sandwiches at lunchtime I ring the mother of a prisoner, Dave, who always worries about him, and also check out a Bourne Trust visitor. Then I go to the Block. The weather is still sunny and three of the men are on exercise so as I pass by the side of the exercise yard I am able to have a nice little chat with them. On occasions like this they are often in good form, and the fact that our conversations are not overheard by officers is a plus for them. They have a joke for me too. Two nuns were driving along when they were stopped by armed robbers. One nun said to the other "Show them your Cross." She opens the window and shouts at them in an angry voice, "Go away this minute or I'll call the police!" She showed them just how cross she was! After attending to my duties in the Block I have coffee and a chat with the cleaners who are prisoners in that part of the establishment for their own protection. They really have very little in the way of recreation, but they still manage a supply of jokes and riddles.

Returning to the wings I ask to see Alan, who has returned there having spent many months in the Block on a charge of bullying. I have known Alan a long time. He's a very big young man with a slight speech impediment which gets more pronounced whenever he gets a bit agitated, and has the effect of making him look quite fierce and intimidating. I feel that he is not a bully but not everyone else shares this opinion. For this reason Alan sometimes has difficulties on the wing, for example in procuring his clothing entitlements, which makes me sometimes wonder who is really the bully? Again, there are no ready answers and none of us knows the full story. I know I want to keep my eye on Alan and his situation.

Dave Holden's Painters and Decorators' workshop is my next destination. Dave is instructor and has just been given a Butler Trust award by Princess Anne in Buckingham Palace – a well-deserved award it is too. I'm dying to hear all about his trip. He tells me that Princess Anne asked his wife Barbara whether he did the painting and decorating at home! Dave is one of those gifted people who has the ability to bring out the best in the prisoners he encounters. How I wish we had many more Dave Holdens in the Prison Service.

Each week for about five weeks now, I've been seeing Gerry for bereavement counselling. Today he sends me a message: "My head's in bits. I can't cope. Can we wait until next week?" I can but respect his wishes and await with interest his story next week.

Patience and energy are beginning to run out. Home beckons. Tomorrow is another day.

19
Prison Officers

Before I joined the prison service as a chaplain I think I would have felt a bit ashamed if any of my family worked in a prison. Even though I had had regular, if very brief, monthly encounters through my visits to Wakefield, I feel that I had quite a lot of prejudice. Maybe this was due to my contact being only with prisoners whose assessments were not always the most objective. I have certainly changed my mind since those days and I have encountered many wonderful and dedicated people who work in prison.

Let me say that not all staff are angels or saints. I have met prisoners who were former prison officers. I have met staff who were bullies and unprofessional. However, there are very few occupations in life which do not have their share of such people. Some have been disgracefully unprofessional and I have felt so angry and sad that they should be the "minders" of the men in prison. During my first week as a prison chaplain I was told by a senior officer that I should never trust a prisoner. Well, I made my own mind up about that piece of advice. I know there are prisoners who can be trusted just as there are some members of staff who cannot be trusted.

It's hard to generalise but on the whole I have found prison officers to be decent people and deserving of far more credit than they are wont to receive from the general public. Their job is often very difficult and unrewarding and it's a job that they do in the name of all of us. Not many people would be prepared to change places with them. Some of the work can be very monotonous and boring, and some of it can be very dangerous when they are dealing with dangerous men. It can be very trying when they are dealing with men who will not or cannot listen, or who should be receiving specialist psychiatric treatment in a psychiatric establishment. On the other hand I have seen some officers who are brilliant and very professional in the way they deal with prisoners and in the respect and dignity they show in their dealings with them. I have seen officers engaging in conversations with prisoners where each treated the other as an equal and no doubt each felt the better for the encounter. I've seen officers making phone calls abroad on behalf of a prisoner who has had a family bereavement, and that takes a lot of time. I've been with officers as we have informed a prisoner of a family bereavement and seen genuine sympathy and concern in their eyes. On one occasion a prison officer and I told one young man of his grandfather's death, and he was devastated. He had been brought up by his grandparents but the last occasion on which he'd seen them was when he had wrecked their house and had to be taken away by the police. I was deeply impressed by the kindness and professionalism shown by the prison officer as we listened to this long story.

I have seen officers approaching governors and writing memos to secure better regimes for the prisoners. The thing that bothers me somewhat, however, is the macho image, which means that although many officers are prepared to be positive in their approach to prisoners they often find it difficult to show their hand in the presence of their colleagues. On the other hand you have officers like Brian, who always appeared to be cheerful, courteous and affirming and who never failed to brighten my day. I really missed him when he retired.

When I first joined the chaplaincy team in Wakefield, a number of officers seemed to take great delight in telling me how evil they considered the prisoners to be, sparing me no details. They also went on to say how odd it was for any woman to be working in such an establishment. They further rubbed it in by saying that if there really was a God then he would surely not have allowed so much suffering in the world. Those early days were not without their difficulties, but thankfully we have got to know each other and to understand each other much better. As I chat with officers now they will often talk about their families or their gardens, their fishing or their music. I have to confess I can never muster up interest in their football! I've noticed that when they focus on life outside the prison they so very often speak of the good things in life for them. They need to do this as life can sometimes be full of tensions at work, tensions that cannot be shared with their families. Indeed there can be many family problems. A prison officer like many other people can have had a bad day at work due to something which he is unable or unwilling to share with his family. He can find on his arrival home that his wife or partner has had a terrible day too and this can often lead to disastrous consequences. On one occasion I was told that an officer had attempted suicide that morning because he had just learnt that his wife was having an affair. I felt really sorry for him but when I went to see him that afternoon I met his wife and was quite amazed at the story she had to tell me. It in no way coincided with the original story I'd heard from the officer himself. On another occasion I met an off-duty officer in town and was amazed at how ill he looked. I stopped to chat and he told me his wife had just thrown him out and he was looking for somewhere to live. About three weeks later I met this same officer at work and asked him how things were. "Never better," was his reply. "I'm now living with another woman and I'm as happy as the days are long." That was quick work! I once asked an officer how he got his broken wrist and was amazed to find that he, whom I'd considered to be one of the most macho men in the prison, was the victim of domestic violence.

Yes, prison officers are often dogged by domestic problems but often they are problems of their own making. I vividly recall the story of Pete. I'd been asked to ring him as he had a big problem. A very worried and anxious Pete said he'd like to meet me, but not close to the prison as he didn't want to be seen. He picked me up at the railway station nearby. I was appalled by the unkempt appearance and distracted look of a man who always dressed smartly. Wanting him to concentrate on the traffic I did not engage in any deep conversation until we were out of town. He then told me about the woman with whom he was having an affair. I still didn't know where we were going but eventually we stopped outside a house and he ran in. I followed, still not knowing whether this was his house or that of his new lady friend. Inside I met an anxious-looking woman who eyed me somewhat suspiciously but offered me coffee which I gladly accepted. I introduced myself and then had to ask her name, which she said was Maria. As I really didn't know Pete very well his wife's name was not known to me so I still didn't know who Maria was! It was an embarrassing situation. Eventually Pete appeared on the scene. It was obvious that Maria was his wife, and we had a good chat. Things were eventually patched up and as far as I know they are still together. People like Pete and Maria are in my prayers daily.

A prison officer who prays a lot might seem like an unlikely individual to encounter. A prison officer who owns up to praying a lot might seem like an even more unlikely person to encounter. A prison officer who works hard on deepening his relationship with God might seem to some a contradiction in terms, and yet in my experience this is not the case. In chats with individual officers they have shared with me the depth of their spirituality and I have been humbled and inspired by that sharing. Granted, I refer here only to a handful of officers but I think of one very senior one, now retired, in particular. One morning he called me into his office on the wing. I assumed it was in connection with the welfare of a prisoner. He then told me that he spent twenty minutes each morning and twenty minutes each evening in prayer. In each case this was a prayer of thanksgiving to God for all his blessings and he wondered whether his prayer was too limited to be acceptable to God. I assured him that I considered this form of prayer to be highly acceptable to God (I didn't even question my own arrogance in speaking on behalf of God!). He also told me that he prayed regularly for the prisoners. Of course he swore me to secrecy that I would never divulge his name – and I haven't – but his story kept me going for a long time.

Reg was a Senior Officer in the Block who was full of personality and had a lively opinion on most matters. On one occasion he and another officer were taking me round the cells to see all the prisoners there. Reg was in very good humour and as he opened one cell he said to the prisoner, "Here is Sr Carmel to bring Jesus to you." As we stood at the door I said, "Hold on, Reg, I don't bring Jesus to Phil, God is already here. He's everywhere." "Now, come on Sister," Reg said, "Jesus was born in Bethlehem and died on Calvary. How can he be here?" At that point we both looked at Phil, the prisoner, seeking his support. With a big grin on his face Phil said, "Don't expect me to give an opinion on this matter. Leave me out of it. I think I'm in enough trouble already." On the way back from the cell I told Reg that henceforth I would consider him to be my theological consultant.

Another occasion which brought a smile to my face was when I went with a prison officer, Graham, to see a sick member of staff who had been off work for many months. He was expecting us but there was no reply when we rang the doorbell. We tried the door and it was open so in we went. There was silence. We thought that maybe he was dead upstairs so Graham began to go upstairs while I, like all good intruders, kept an eye on the window. I then saw our sick friend approaching the house and we both scuttled out as if we'd been up to no good! Our sick friend had gone out to get some milk for our coffee.

Without doubt, one of the greatest things I have noticed about prison officers is the way they help and support each other when there is a real difficulty.

This does not necessarily always extend to the day-to-day routine work in the prison but when there is a crisis or sickness I have found them to be amazingly supportive, not just to their colleague who is in trouble of whatever kind, but also to his family. I have seen them give of their time and their skills without stint. On many occasions I have accompanied Colin, who had responsibilities in the POA, on such missions. On one occasion the wife of a prison officer who we often visited called us "the terrible twins".

Personally, I've always been aware that when I've been out and about throughout the prison, prison staff have looked after me well. No wonder I think well of them.

20

Peru and Florida

O n my bedroom wall hangs a beautiful tapestry which never fails to give me hope no matter how depressing the circumstances in Wakefield or indeed elsewhere. This tapestry depicts a beautiful cuddly white lamb sitting on the lap of a brown lion. Beside them is a brilliant yellow sunflower with a bright red centre and bright green leaves. On the top of the tapestry in bold letters is the word PAZ (peace). This magnificent piece of work was done by a prisoner, Pedro, in the midst of the most appalling and squalid conditions in the main prison in Lima, and was given to me when I visited there some years ago.

At that time I had been on a pastoral visit to our Sisters in Peru. A sister from another congregation, Brigid, who was a nurse, was very involved in prison ministry. She kindly agreed to take me in with her, and what an extraordinary visit that was.

As we approached the prison in her little car I asked Brigid if I might take a photo of the outside of the prison. I was already reaching for my camera but she said no. At that very minute two guards appeared in front of us, pointing their guns at us. Needless to say I hastily pushed the camera back into my bag and then pushed the bag well under the car seat. Brigid, who had made the necessary arrangements for my visit, explained to them who I was and in we went. Apparently most of the prison guards were on strike, and the police were taking their place. Strikes were almost the order of the day in Peru at that time and during that particular week doctors and nurses were also on strike. There was great security, and I was introduced as the Mother General of Brigid's Order. The staff were not very friendly – in fact quite the contrary. I noticed a big picture of Our Lady Help of Christians in the office. I thought of how different it was to any picture I might see in a Wakefield office and how different the attitude of the staff there from the friendly attitude I find amongst Wakefield staff.

When we got into the campus, there was a huge open area thronging with prisoners who came flocking up to us showing us all sorts of hideous open sores, especially on their legs. Some of those sores were bleeding and had flies all round them. They all had dirty clothes and very few had shoes. They knew Brigid was a nurse and she had been given permission to bring some basic medicines in as no doctors or nurses were available that week. She also gave those who flocked round half a bar of soap each, telling me that what they really needed was a good wash. I gather that it was only possible for them to collect their daily supply of water, in whatever containers they had, from about 6.00 to 6.30 each morning. The heat was overpowering, as was the bad smell which got even worse when we went inside one of the thirteen pavilions. Inside, there were villainous-looking men hanging around everywhere and dirt and dogs and squalor abounding. There were no prison guards to be seen but I gathered a few were about somewhere and if a prisoner did something wrong then he could be shot on the spot. Most of the prisoners looked undernourished.

We walked to the chaplaincy which was a real oasis – clean and bright and cheerful. Here we met a number of trusted prisoners, one of whom had made my tapestry of the lion and lamb at peace. It was lovely to see so much creative work being done there and also work with men who were trying to come off drugs. Brigid had told me that about 90 percent of the people in the prison were on drugs. From the chaplaincy we walked to the prison hospital and had to wait outside until the door was unlocked by a prisoner. I was amazed to find how many of the prisoners carried keys. They have a far more active role in the running of the prison than I could ever have imagined. As I was looking round, a smartly dressed Frenchman was admitted by the key-holding prisoner. This Frenchman spoke excellent English. He was a priest who lectured in philosophy in the nearby university and often visited the prison on his day off, bringing some basic medical supplies.

As I conversed with him, prisoners were bringing bundles into the hospital which were also extremely dirty. At one point I noticed four prisoners carrying a particularly heavy bundle. My curiosity overcame me and I looked to see what they were carrying. To my horror I saw it was a dead man they had picked up outside. I felt quite sick and immediately averted my eyes, but there I met another terrible sight – a man lying on the floor with blood oozing from the many open sores on his legs. Medicine was not available. We moved along and met one young man with his leg heavily bandaged. He had received gunshot wounds the night before in a shoot-out in the prison! Amazingly he looked happy and this was because he was having his first court hearing the following day after being on remand for five and a half years. I later heard that the lawyers were on strike the following day. The heat was stifling for the whole of the time we were there from 9.30am to 2.30pm and on no occasion did I see any food being given to the prisoners. We went to visit a cell which was shared by four prisoners who were sitting on the floor making baskets or mats. The toilet facilities were primitive in the extreme and the smell was overpowering.

Paperwork was all-important in the prison set-up. Even if a man had finished his sentence he would not be allowed his freedom until all the necessary paperwork was completed. The Sisters did a lot to help the men in this regard and I greatly admired all that was done by the chaplains. I was very glad to leave that prison behind me. When I returned to Wakefield I told the men that their prison was like Buckingham Palace in comparison, but this was not an opinion that went down very well with them.

Another prison which I visited more recently was located in Florida. I managed that visit while on a trip to my nephew Brian on the occasion of his ordination to the deaconate in the USA. My visit to the prison was arranged by a volunteer called Vince. At this prison I saw very little sign of keys as the doors and gates we went through were opened and locked electronically. I felt at home with the prisoners who were friendly like those of Wakefield. However, I did not feel at home with the staff, but found them very intimidating. As I walk through Wakefield I usually say hello to everyone I meet, whether staff, prisoners or visitors. The staff at this prison, however, instead of returning my greeting as people do at Wakefield, looked at me almost as if I had two heads. The smiles I received from them were very few and far between and I found that chaplaincy facilities were indeed limited. Most of the prisoners I saw were black – which told its own story in that setting. Vince brought me to see a middle-aged man called Charlie whose trial was due to begin the following week. Charlie was expected to receive the death penalty and I cringed as I looked at him and thought about it. We then went to see Jim who, in his mid-twenties, was due to be released the following week. Jim's father had been on Death Row for 10 years, his uncle had been on Death Row for a year and his mother was in a neighbouring women's prison for stabbing someone. What chance did poor Jim have? I was particularly saddened to see so many fourteen to seventeen-year-old boys whose eyes had already lost their sparkle. In the women's area too there was a lifelessness about the prisoners. However, even in such a place – as everywhere – there is hope. A lovely young woman prisoner called Sherry told me she had recently found peace and had found God through her poetry. She gave me a poem she had written the previous day, of which one verse ran something like this:

> *My life has been nothing but sorrow and shame*
> *But now is the time to get rid of that game,*
> *No more shadows hovering over me with gloom,*
> *Because now I'm God's flower just starting*
>   *to bloom.*

I was impressed by the drugs strategy and the number of drugs counsellors whom I met there. I was also favourably impressed by the food which I saw being served. Leaving the women's area, we passed by a gym. I was pleasantly surprised to see it and asked how often the prisoners were allowed to use it. I was told in no uncertain terms that the gym was for the use of staff and not prisoners. The idea behind that prohibition for prisoners was that the gym would make them more fit and consequently more dangerous. Thank God that is not the philosophy which operates in Wakefield, where the idea is that prisoners can let off steam in the gym and consequently get rid of a lot of aggression. On the same campus as the prison was a local courthouse and also the mayor's offices. The contrast between the two areas could not be more striking. In the luxury of his office I had a chat with a man who appeared to have a very senior post in the management structure of the prison. Among the questions I asked him was one concerning the conditions for visitors in the prison. He spoke of his brilliant new idea. Visitors would remain outside the prison and the "visit" would take place as both prisoner and visitor sat in front of their separate monitors rather than seeing each other face to face. There would be no physical contact – not even a handshake. I thought of the sadness for families and especially for mothers and I felt so glad that I had never heard such an idea being put forward in this country. If only all of us, in whatever country we live, could help to forge and support family links, how much less crime-ridden our society would be.

As Vince and I were leaving the prison a very angry, abrupt and rude guard was questioning a visitor who had just arrived at the gate. I have never seen such a lack of courtesy in an English prison. To add insult to injury Vince told me that the guard's name was Murphy and I felt ashamed that he bore a name which is so common in my own country.

Visiting that prison was an interesting experience but I was glad to leave it and all the more determined to highlight that bit of our prison statement which says "Our duty is to treat them with humanity". There is always hope. Miracles still happen. The lion and the lamb can still lie down in peace, and just before I turn off my light in my bedroom at night I can wink at the lion and lamb on that lovely tapestry on my wall, and in my heart say "Lord, I know you'll look after Ian or Steve or Terry or Charlie or Reg, or John or Asher or Mahomet. We are all in the hollow of your hand."

21

Joy and Sorrow

Arriving at the prison this morning I saw to my dismay a fire engine outside. As I got closer I saw two other fire engines. Then they moved away. It was a false alarm – thank God. I dread to think of how it would be if there was a major fire, though the prison is well prepared. When the fire alarm goes in any part of the prison the signal is received at the fire station and the engines are on their way immediately. The prison pays the bill – and it must be a mighty big one – but it's good to know such precaution is taken to ensure everybody's safety. I was the only person in the chaplaincy on one occasion when the fire alarm went and after quickly grabbing my coat – it was a very cold day – I went outside. Above the chaplaincy is the gym so I was soon joined by several of the prisoners and their instructor and we spent the time telling jokes. I got several offers for the loan of my warm coat but I selfishly declined them all! It was an entertaining, if cold, twenty minutes and thank God there was no fire. But let me return to today.

I went first to see Jason who is due to be released tomorrow and he was very happy indeed though a bit apprehensive. I'd spoken with his father about two weeks ago and he was even more apprehensive. I recall some years ago when a middle-aged man, Martin, was due to be released. He was so frightened at the prospect of going out and facing the world that he actually locked himself in his cell so as to delay his departure. I can only hope and pray that all goes well for Jason. He absolutely loved Irish music so hopefully he will find that a useful therapy. On leaving his wing I had a little word with John, newly arrived in Wakefield – yet again. John first came into prison in 1949 and has seen very little of the outside world in all that time in between. He is the essence of politeness and courtesy, despite whatever offences he has committed to keep him in custody for so long.

I was still reflecting on John's situation as I made my way to see Stewart, who has been suicidal during these last few days. The main reason for this was that he had received a "Dear John" letter from his wife saying that their marriage was over. Stewart felt it was all his fault as he was constantly discouraging her from doing anything for herself or taking the two children to any interesting places. He realised he was far too selfish and possessive and lacking in trust and he now has to pay the price. It's a sad situation. There are many like Stewart who in their own way try to impose a prison sentence on their partners.

I've been concerned for some time about the position regarding letters in the prison. Prisoners are graded as either basic, standard or enhanced regarding the privileges they receive. If a man is on basic then he is not allowed to be in possession of a postage stamp though he is entitled to send a prison letter each week. If a prisoner is in the Healthcare Centre or the Block and his friend back on the wing wishes to write to him or vice versa then the letters have to be sent out of the prison in the post and come back into the prison in the post. To my way of thinking this is a terrible waste of money, considering the fact that the prisoners have so little cash. I approached the relevant governor to ask if this ruling could be reconsidered especially in the light of the fact that we have an excellent internal mail system. The answer I got was no. I thought, as I have done many times before, "Thank God it's not payment by results for me." No wonder I'm not a rich woman.

My next call was to the library to see if I could borrow a book for myself on basic computer skills as I am computer illiterate and wish to remedy that situation. I didn't get a book but I found two prisoners who were willing to give me my first lesson. In their little room where they produce the prison magazine *The Mulberry Bush*, Nigel and Ken taught me how to produce a little card which reads "Hi, how are you?" on the front and "Carmel" on the reverse. That little card is my pride and joy and the production of it gave a lightness to my step for the rest of the day.

During the lunch break I snatched a few minutes to put the final touches to my talk on my work in Wakefield to be given to a group of ladies in Halifax next Monday evening.

It was with some sadness that I went to Greg's workshop in the afternoon. I'd spoken at great length with him yesterday. He's due to be released very soon but as his case is extremely high profile it will be very difficult for him to find somewhere to live where he will be left in peace. He talked at length about himself and his background and his offences which he did not seek to minimise at all. He was disturbed by false statements made in the media which make his situation even more difficult. He feels that the only real solution to his problem would be for him to have a sex change but this would not appear to be a likely solution from the Home Office point of view. He told me he had experienced some difficulty in his workshop (it's amazing what a definite pecking order there is among prisoners) and it was for this reason that I made my way there. He was not there, having been admitted to the hospital. When Greg had gone to his cell at lunchtime having collected his meal, he found that someone had been in during his absence and smashed his radio and his flask. The future looks bleak for poor Greg.

If the future looks bleak for Greg today, it certainly looks better for Richard. When I went into the Visits room he introduced me to his dad. I remarked on the striking similarity in their appearance and then discovered that they were meeting for the first time in 26 years. Richard was only two years old at that time. Both were very much looking forward to the prospect of getting to know each other even if they were a little apprehensive. I hope it all works out well for them.

There was plenty for me to think about on my way home. "Joyful or sorrowful, nothing will last." However, my little computer card and the joy of making it will stay with me for a long time.

22
Special Memories

Thinking of special memories gives me a big problem – that of selection. So many things that happen in Wakefield are so very special that it really is difficult to make a selection so I am just going to describe them at random.

I think of Bob, who complained that the hot cross buns which the men got on Good Friday were unacceptable to him as he was not a Christian, but who still ate one. I think of Jim who complained because a Muslim was eating a pork chop in the kitchen (I might well have done the same if I'd been in his shoes and had the opportunity). I think of Mike who ordered ten red roses for a friend. When I commented that she must be a very special lady he informed me that she was his first wife and he had had four since – but none as nice as she was. I think of the two men, considered highly dangerous, who were in our most secure accommodation in the Block. After leaving Wakefield one of them wrote to me and said "You know, I miss me old cage" (a tribute to the professionalism of the staff who were looking after him). The other wrote in our prison magazine, "I have no money, no property, no rights and no worries." It always amazed me that he could be so much at peace with himself.

I think of Tom whom I had never seen in church but who came along during Holy Week. Thinking it might be an anniversary I asked him if there was a special reason for him coming down. His reply was, "Yes, there is – my Saviour died for me." I think of Fred who told me that what he most missed in prison was seeing the stars and not feeling the sun or breeze on his face. I think of Neil who told me he was fed up with the "God business" and that church didn't work for him at all! On one occasion I did an in-depth interview with him and at the end he said he'd never before talked so long without swearing! I think of another in-depth interview with a man called Mike who was serving several life sentences. In the middle of the interview he gave a great shout and then jumped up on to the chair and then on to the table. I was somewhat taken aback but had to smile when I discovered that the cause of his sudden terror was a humble little bumble bee. I think of the prison officer I accompanied as he tried to trace his mother: when finally an address was found, he discovered that she had died six months previously. I think of Bernie, doing a life sentence for the death of his daughter, who every year arranges for flowers to be in chapel with the note "To Ann, from your loving father. I will always love you". I know he does! I think of Tony who met his fiancée in a little room at the back of the visiting area on a Tuesday. He was at the very beginning of a life sentence but that Tuesday was his birthday and also the very day on which he was due to marry his fiancée. I think of Terry who told me that the difference between an RC and a C of E prisoner was that the C of E man wore a cross and chain and the RC wore "rosemary" beads. I think of Timothy who said he would have preferred the death penalty to the mental torture of doing a life sentence. He told me he was contemplating suicide because life was a real hell. I think of Con, a trustee prisoner who I let through an inside gate because I didn't like to see him waiting in the rain. He said, "I'm in no hurry. I have 91 years left so a few minutes don't matter." (A life sentence is considered to be 99 years.) On another occasion I was walking round the exercise yard with Con and it was very cold. I suggested to him that we walk more briskly. He said, "What for? It will get me nowhere." On another occasion still, I was telling him how difficult it was to get in through the prison gate that morning. "You should try getting out," he said. What a deep impression all these little incidents made on me!

I will never forget the time I pressed the alarm bell during my very first week at Wakefield. Alarm bells are to be found all over the prison. During my first days I had an awful lot of learning to do. One morning I wanted to make a phone call but I accidentally touched the alarm button. I immediately realised what I had done and just froze momentarily to the spot. By the time I got to the door to say it was a mistake I was horrified to see running in my direction, from north, south, east and west and even up the steps, a multitude of officers. I was embarrassed beyond words but it certainly broke the ice for me and provided an entertaining conversation point for the week. I can assure you it never happened to me again. Another embarrassing occasion was when I got locked in the loo at the end of one of the wings. It was during the lunch break when the prisoners were locked in their cells and there was a minimum of officers on duty. Try as I might, I failed to unlock the door with my key. I banged on the door but was ignored by the officer in the nearby office who said he thought it was a noisy prisoner. (I had something to say to him about that later on!) It was some time later that I heard someone come through the wing gate. I banged and shouted again, and thankfully an officer came to my rescue. That too was an incident that they did not let me forget in a hurry.

Writing letters for prisoners has been for me a rather special part of my ministry. Jimmy, a middle-aged man, asked me to write a letter for him to his mother. Jimmy had no idea what he wanted me to write but nodded his approval as I made suggestions. At the end I handed him my biro to add his signature but he seemed very reluctant. Not realising the reason for his reluctance I pressed him further and found that he was laboriously writing his surname. It was only then that it dawned on me that he was unable to write Jimmy, so I wrote it for him on a piece of paper and this he slowly copied. As I was about to retrieve my biro he started to put kisses on every available space on that sheet of paper. I would say it was a very happy mother indeed who received that letter.

Phil also had great difficulty in writing letters to his mother. He was a very young prisoner still trying to come to terms with his sentence. He was greatly amused on one occasion as he dictated his letter to find that I had some difficulty in spelling the word 'gerbil'. The following week he was dictating a letter and wanted to use the word 'recommendation'. "Oh Sister," he said, "you're in real trouble here and I can't help you. If you can't spell 'gerbil', how will you manage 'recommendation'?" He had the habit of approaching me just as I was about to leave the wing to go back to the chaplaincy for my sandwich. When I said this to him once, he told everybody whom he met that afternoon that I thought more of my sandwich than I did of him. Some you win, some you don't.

Then there are the letters I've written for Paul. These are to his Gran, whose letters I read to him and which are full of affection for him. She is in poor health and her big worry is that she might not still be alive when he comes out of prison. She says that every time she thinks of him she cries. Paul is a great supporter of Newcastle so we always have a paragraph in the letter about Alan Shearer and how the team is getting on. In a recent letter Gran had the sad news that Sam the dog had died. On that occasion Paul had plenty of material for our reply to the letter. He spoke at length of how he had cried when he heard that Sam had died. It reminded him of very happy times in the past when he and Sam were out chasing rabbits and the hours of fun they had together. When I think of Paul and many like him doing life sentences I reflect on the fact that their moments of violence, compared with the whole of the rest of their lives were very few, though the consequences were so tragic and so enormous.

My concluding special memory has inspired me many a time. Some years ago, as already mentioned, we had a big Mission in Wakefield. One of the leaders was a magician and on one occasion when his theme was "Putting our Trust in God" he used a large knife and a carrot. When, despite appearances to the contrary, the carrot remained untouched by the knife, he invited a volunteer from the congregation to put his arm in the same position as the carrot had been in. He then invited him to put his trust in the man holding the knife. Naturally, the volunteer's arm was not cut off, but in the meantime the carrot was just discarded. During our Prisoners' Week Service that same year, the theme was "Picking up the Pieces". Alan, a prisoner, led our service. In his homily he referred to the knife and carrot episode but what Alan highlighted moved me very deeply. He referred to Tony, a chaplain, who had retrieved the discarded carrot, taken it home and used it to make a delicious carrot cake which he brought in the following Sunday afternoon and shared with the men. He had "picked up the pieces" in a very simple and lovely way and to me that was a parable of life in Wakefield. He had used a situation, useless and insignificant though it seemed to bring a little bit of joy and peace into the lives of the men. May God bless Tony for what he did and may God bless Alan for having the eyes to see, the ears to hear, and the wisdom to be able to share the experience with the rest of us.

23

The Future

Today, 25 April 1999, is a very special day for me. Forty years ago today I made my vows as a Sister of Mercy. It's a day for looking back and I thank God for all that has been. It's a day for looking forward too and in the middle of next month I'll be 60 years old – certainly a landmark! During the time of writing this book I have thought about the future and as I approach 60 I feel the need to have my batteries recharged and my energy renewed. I am therefore retiring from Wakefield Prison on my 60th birthday.

As I reflected on this and prayed very much about it I wondered how life would be for me without Wakefield. I felt it would be a life with a huge gap in it. Life can often be without smooth endings. I suppose my dream would have been to remain in Wakefield Prison until I could go on no further but I don't feel that that is what the good Lord has in store for me. I was always lucky in that I had freedom to respond to any situation where I saw the need. I've been accustomed to keeping my eyes and ears wide open, and of course my mind and heart as well. I feel that the best we can give to anyone is ourselves. To me it was an advantage, difficult though it seemed at times, not being able to give material things to the men. They understood the situation and so there was freedom to give them what could only be freely given: energy, compassion and love. No matter what the financial cuts, restrictions could not be made in this area. Just being able to be alongside those men in their heart-break, their depression, their anger, anxiety and frustration, and their experience of seeing no light whatever at the end of the tunnel, was a privileged position to be in. But it wasn't all darkness. There was usually joy to be found somewhere, maybe in a relationship mended or a good exam result achieved or a new talent discovered. It was good to be there with them for these times.

On my desk today is an anniversary card from my dear friend Beryl which depicts a most beautiful scene of bluebells and azaleas between which runs a lovely little path. She observes: "Just round the corner the path will be taking you through to new beginnings – almost a fresh start". Also on my desk is a card from one of the Sisters in my Community, Monica, on the front of which is written: "I sought my soul, the soul I could not see. I sought my God and he eluded me. I sought my brother and found all three."

The men of Wakefield Prison have been and are my brothers and I am so pleased to be their sister. Who knows what the future holds? I quote the words of my father: "God has never let us down and you can be sure that he will always look after us." That continues to fill me with great confidence for the future – a future full of hope.

My last week in Wakefield provided me with what I know will be very special and endearing memories.

In many ways it was "business as usual" – that's what I like best – but it also had many highlights. In a way, my feet never touched the ground that week. It was full of sadness in saying "Goodbye" so many times, but one thing is for sure, I have never been kissed by so many men in such a short space of time and who could complain about that?

I felt flattered but humbled that the BBC came into the prison to film a news item for "Look North". The best part of it for me was being able to say to such a wide audience what niceness and goodness there still is in the prisoners in Wakefield. It amused me somewhat to find that the part the producer seemed to highlight was the occasion when I kissed a prisoner. On behalf of the men in his workshop he had presented me with a magnificent painting, a beautifully coloured Celtic design with the words: "O Night divine, O Night when Christ was born". This is already forming a beautiful centrepiece for our Millennium area in the convent. On the morning following that particular "Look North" programme I was at the bus stop as usual at 7.00am. As I stepped on to the No. 110 bus with its silent passengers the driver greeted me with a big smile and in a loud voice said, "Good morning, sweetheart. I saw you on TV last night and you were great." Well, that made my day – just one of the many things that made my day. The *Yorkshire Evening Post* later wrote an article on some of my memories of Wakefield and that too moved some very old friends and acquaintances of mine to get in touch – another delightful experience.

Throughout the week I had many cards and messages and was at the receiving end of so much love and support and affirmation. What particularly touched me were the cards from men who have great

138

difficulty with writing and written communication made their messages very precious indeed.

We had a service in chapel one evening which had me in tears. It was arranged by Fr Malachy and even though this was not the phrase that the men would use I found I was "being missioned" by them. I quote liberally from the text of this service because I feel that it was a huge bridge between my past and my future. They said to me: "As you experience the pain of change and the insecurity of moving on, we pray that you may also experience the blessing of inner growth. As you meet the poor, the pained and the stranger on the Way, we pray that you may see in each one the face of Christ. As you walk through the good times and the bad we pray that you may never lose sight of the shelter of God's love. As you ponder your decisions and wonder over the fruits of your choice, we pray that the peace of Christ may reign in your heart."

Their final prayer was: "Shelter Carmel from all harm and anxiety. Grant her courage to meet the future, grace to let go of the past and embrace her new life, through Christ our Lord. Amen."

I am full of confidence that those prayers are heard. Following the service we chatted around and I was very touched indeed as individual prisoners came along to mention their special memory – a particular moment in our encounter and a very joyful and humbling experience for me. Following the service the chaplains took me out for a meal which I thoroughly enjoyed. I have always been happy to avail myself of any opportunity to celebrate.

On the last Thursday we had a presentation by the Governor at lunchtime. The Centre was full of officers and other staff. As I walked down the steps the

Governor said, with a smile, "Don't trip or you'll spoil the scene." I'd been quaking with fright but that made me chuckle. Amazingly I didn't trip. At the word of command from my dear old friend, Principal Officer Mick, the officers stood to attention. I couldn't get over it. The only woman I'd ever seen getting such attention was the President of Ireland. It was an amazing experience and what words I heard of the Governor's talk seemed to refer to someone else, not me. I got some beautiful flowers and my "discharge paper" which was signed by the Governor and said that I had successfully completed my sentence with an EDR of 13 May 1999. EDR means 'earliest date of release' and the inclusion of that means that I could be recalled – so who knows!

That night the officers put on a buffet in the club – and a lovely one it was too. It was just a pity that all the excitement had taken my appetite away. I really appreciated their thoughtfulness in bringing along an Irish band, and of course I loved the flowers I received. Words fail me to express adequately the surprise and delight I felt when I was told that the prison is sponsoring a bed in my name at Wakefield Hospice. That was a great, great joy for me to know.

I began my last morning as usual with the 7.45am Mass at St Austin's. Here another beautiful surprise was in store. Mass was said for me and afterwards I was brought next door for a second breakfast – this time tea and a delicious bacon buttie which I thoroughly enjoyed. My intention was to spend my last hours in Wakefield just walking round the old haunts – a kind of pilgrimage. I found, however, that I had no need to do that. Wakefield has been written – indelibly I feel – in my heart and mind and soul.

A few days after leaving Wakefield I called on our local newsagent, Marie, to say thank you for keeping me extra copies of the *Yorkshire Evening Post* containing the above-mentioned article. As I came out on to Hunslet Road the No. 110 bus was passing on its way to Wakefield. I recognised the driver who at that moment caught my eye and gave me a big wave. I returned that wave and felt it was a gesture symbolising my goodbye to Wakefield.

The future is indeed full of hope. Soon I go to Rome with other Sisters who are celebrating 40 years of religious profession. One of the many things I'm looking forward to there is meeting up with Sr Madeleine who first introduced me to prison life many, many years ago. I think we'll be burning the midnight oil on a few occasions during that visit as we reminisce and recall the happy, the sad, the funny and the extraordinary happenings in Wakefield over the years.

I hope to take a sabbatical in the United States so that I can recharge the batteries and renew the energy, and as the prisoners have ordered me to "take time to chill out too" this I certainly intend to do. It should be no problem. I hope to do a renewal course in New York State and a highlight for me should be to see that part of the world in the Fall. My nephew has invited me to spend Christmas with him in Florida and I hope to be there for the Millennium celebrations too, following which I would like to do some study in Florida together with some pastoral work. Dare I say it? I have a really strong wish that this pastoral work will include prison ministry of some description. After that, who knows? Maybe I'll end up in jail again. At this moment I cannot think of anything else that would make me more happy than that.